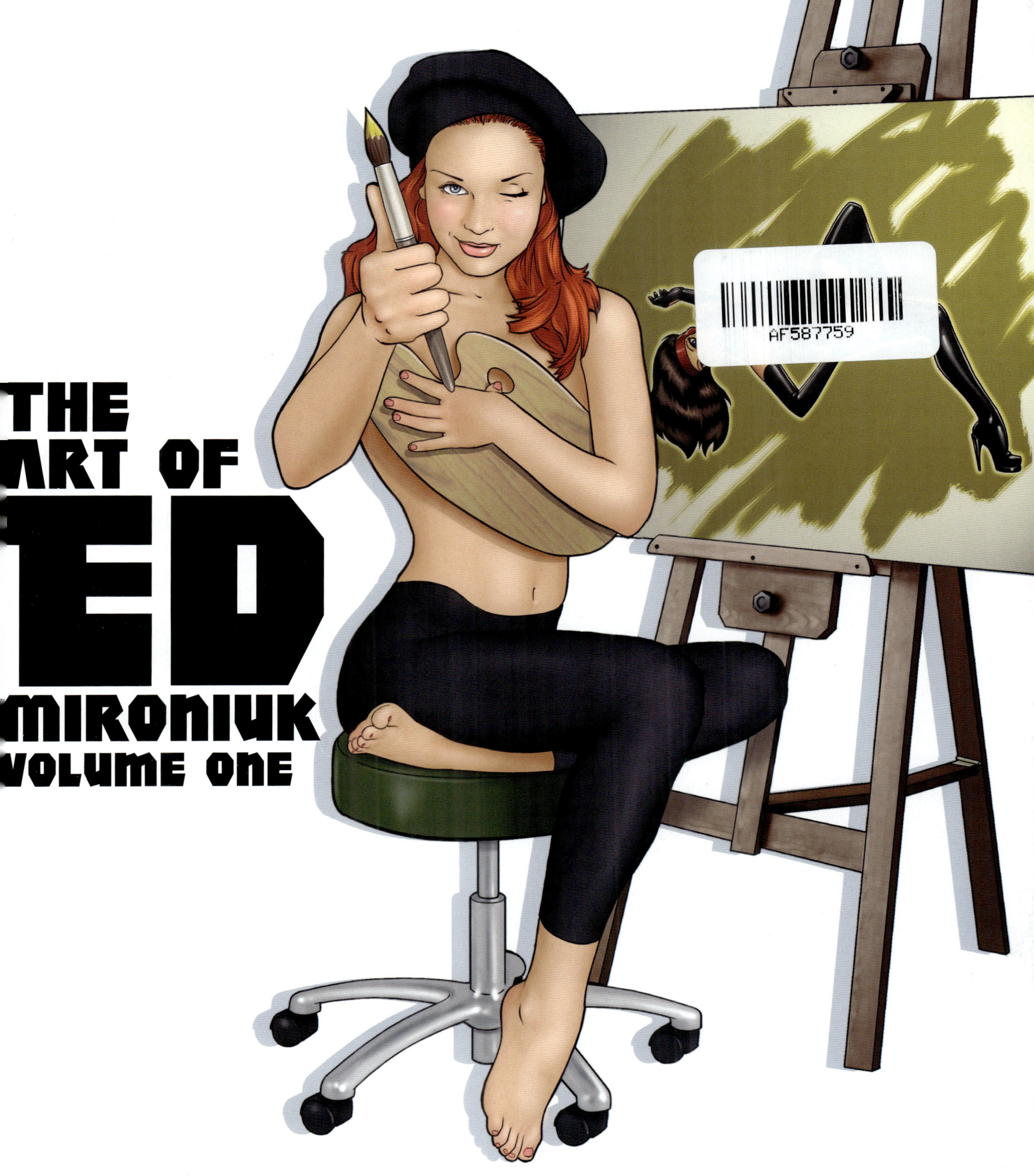

AN SQP PRESENTATION

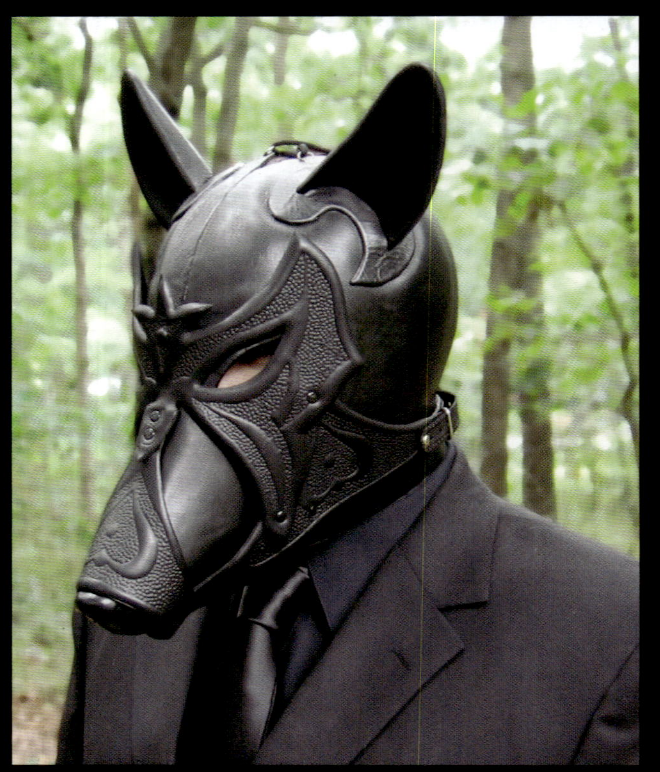

Ed Mironiuk entered our world on Dec 11th, 1969 in the improbable setting of Buffalo, NY. His singular and strange nature quickly convinced his parents that one child would be enough, as they never had another. He began drawing in earnest as soon as his tender fingers could grip a pencil and put it to paper. Edgar Rice Burroughs, Frazetta, sci fi and comics (most especially, his beloved Conan) consumed his time and encouraged his fetid imagination. By the age of 12 he discovered Alberto Vargas through an inherited collection of musty Playboys, perhaps the only pre-pubescent to truly appreciate pornography on an esoteric level. This early admiration of the female form would serve as the foundation of his later artwork. While normal kids were drawing hotrods and wondering how to get into the girl next door's pants, Ed was memorializing what was actually IN the girl next door's pants through detailed illustrations.

After a decent run in high school, Ed hightailed it out of Central New York and went straight to his muse – NYC's East Village. He drank his way through 4 years at Parson's School of Design and managed to come away with a BFA, despite his predilection for tequila. While Ed toiled away at mundane illustration and animation jobs, he fed his head a steady diet of black metal, Russ Meyer films, HP Lovecraft, latex fashion, ink and piercings of all natures and the absolute vilest sectors of Japanese deviancies. These subcultures stewed in his brain and eventually merged with his love of pinups, forming the basis of his unique brand of art; a hybrid of pop trash and fetish culture kissed by Dr. Moreau himself. In 1993 he was anointed reigning illustrator for Tattoo Magazine, a role he still kicks ass at. It was during this time that Ed met Kristin Tercek, the only woman who could kick the tequila bottle out of his hand so he could use it to craft his art. They quickly married and started Cha-Pow!, an animation ink and paint company that is still thriving and well known for its work on MTV, Nickelodeon, and Saturday Night Live. Since then, they've expanded their empire into custom made dolls and Ed's illustration work has been featured in everything from The LA Times to Equus Eroticus and used for bands as diverse as The Genitorturers and SPiT LiKE THiS. Ed throws all this work into the world from his cocoon in the boondocks of Jersey, where he lives with his loving wife and needy Chihuahuas.

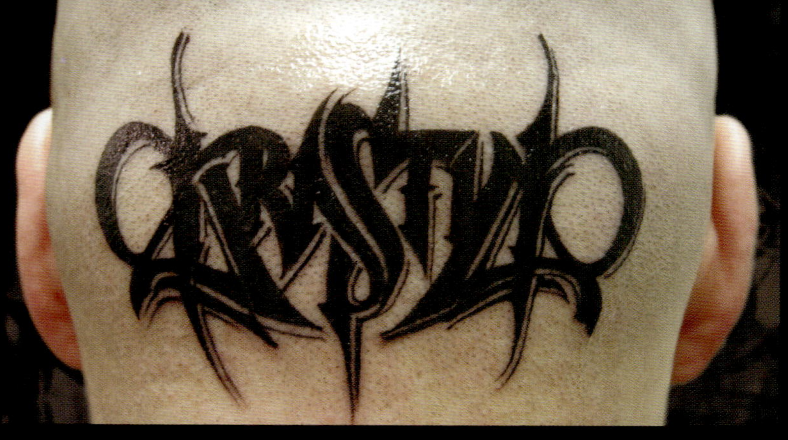

This book is dedicated to my wife and partner in crime Kris.

- Ed Mironiuk

For the very latest on all things Mironiuk, go to:
www.edmironiuk.com

The Art of Ed Mironiuk

 Printed in China.
Book design by Grassy Knoll Studios.

Published by
SQP Inc.
PO Box 248 - Columbus, NJ 08022

Sal Quartuccio & Bob Keenan - Publishers

For a free full color catalog showcasing the entire SQP line of erotic, fantasy, and pin-up artwork, go to:
www.sqpinc.com

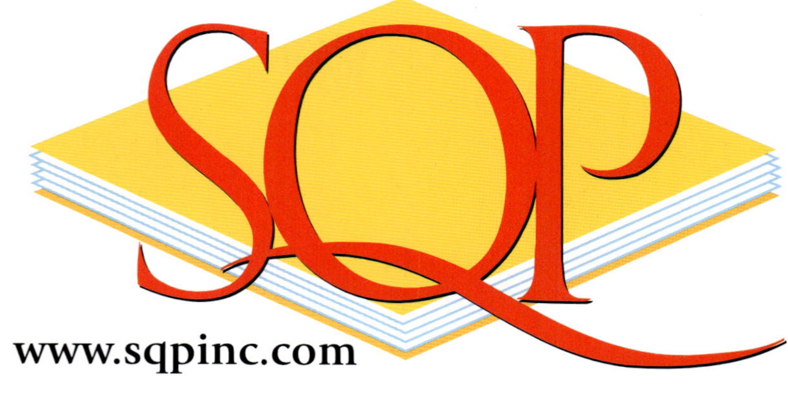

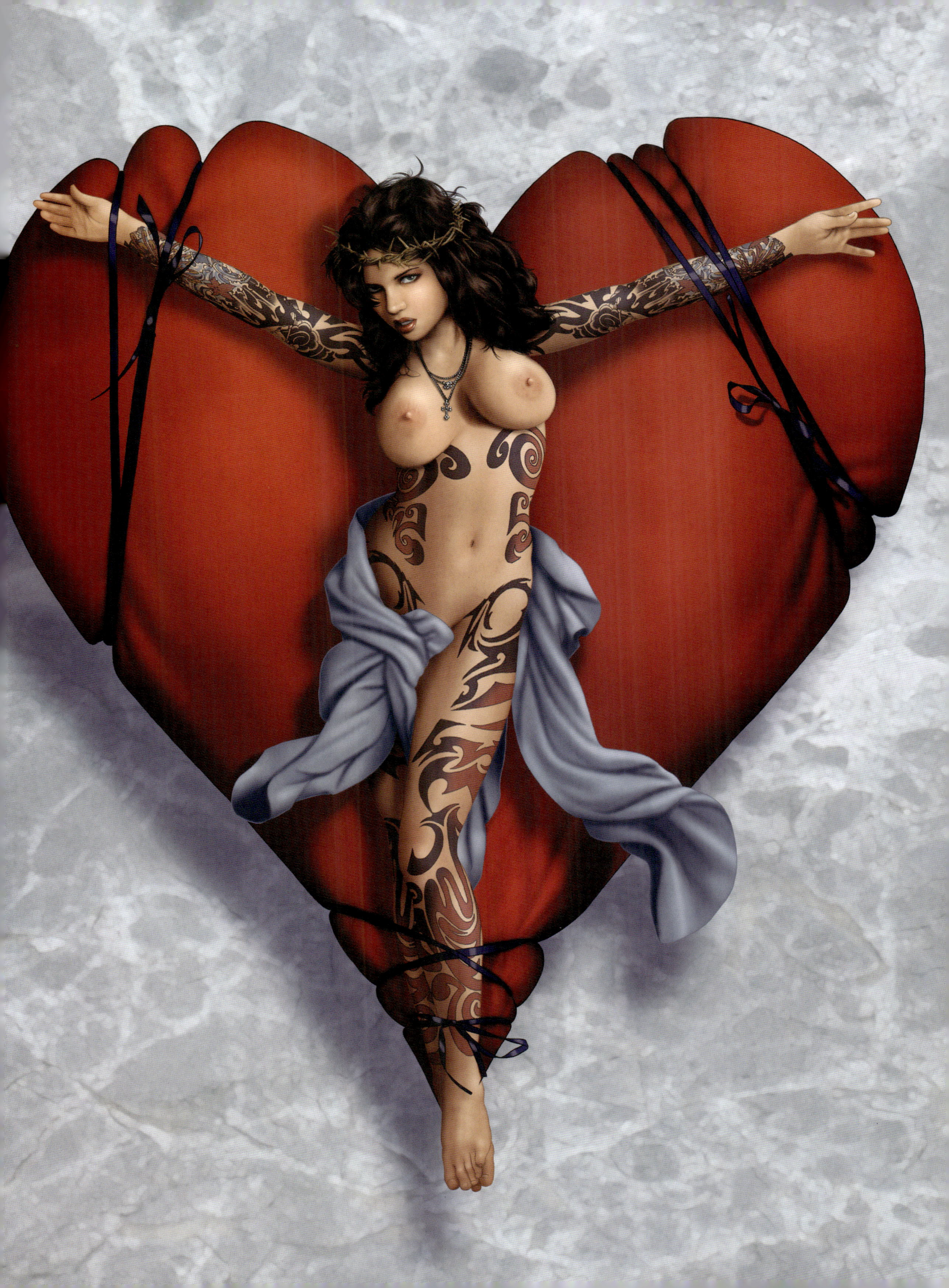

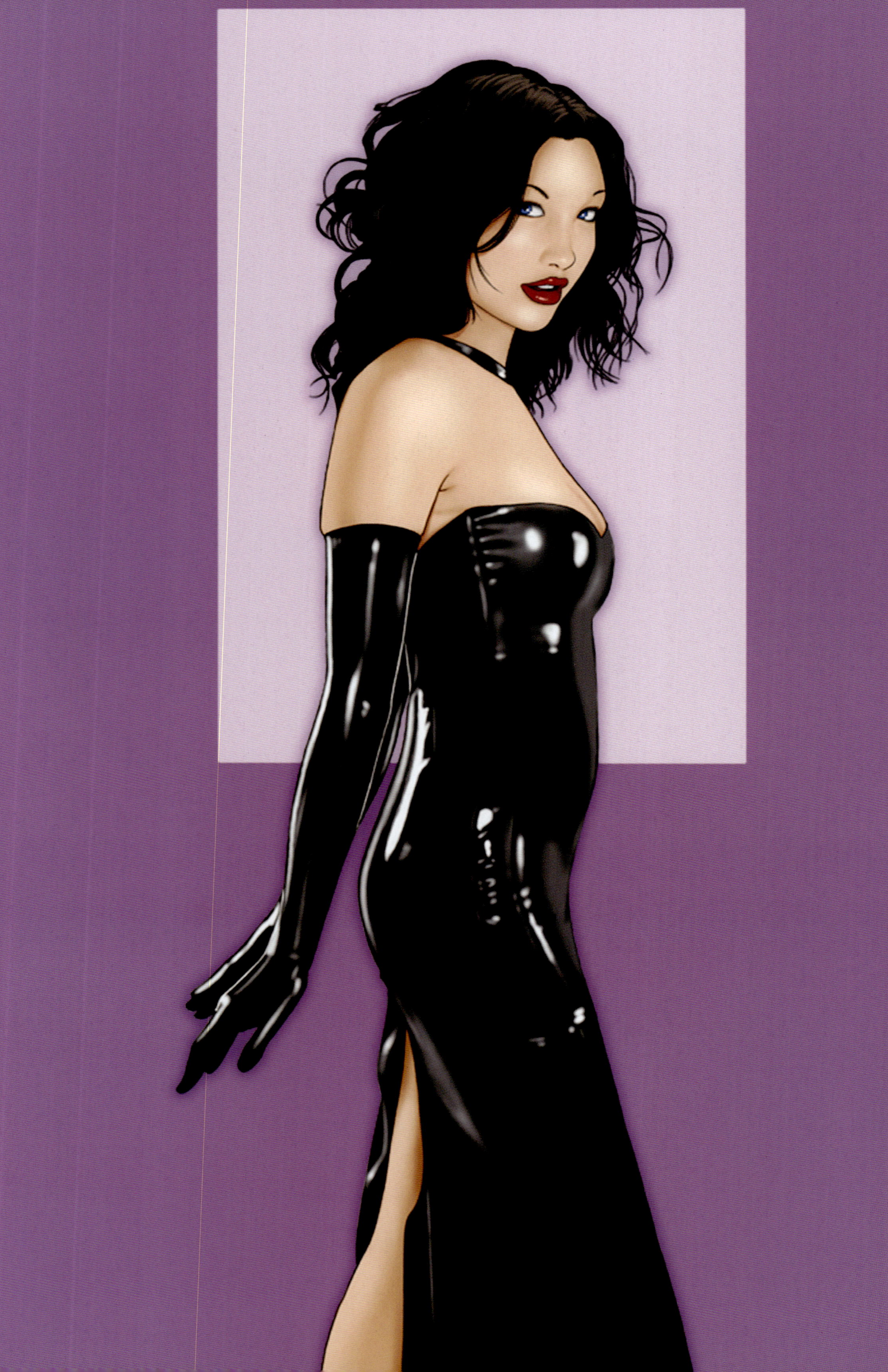

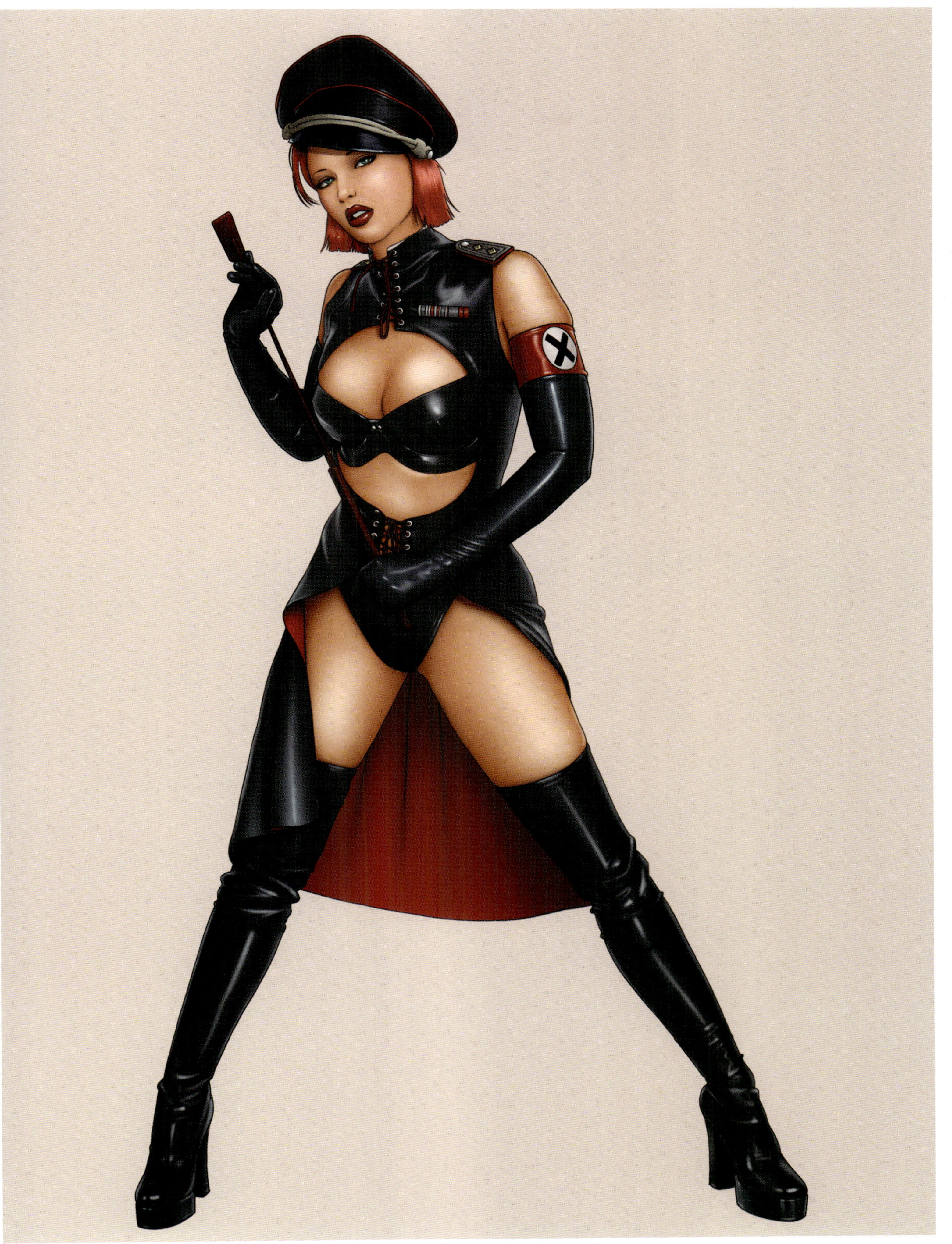

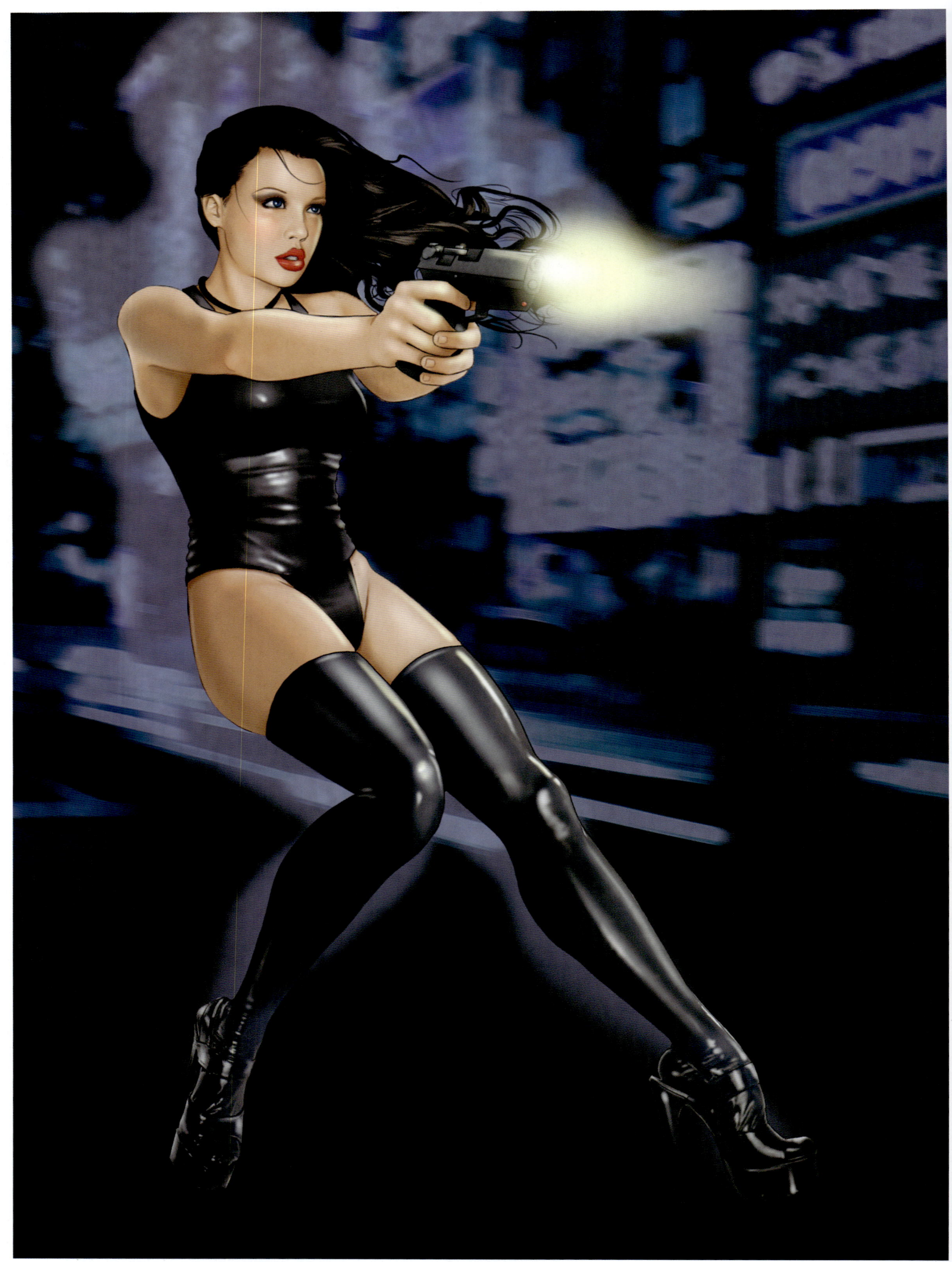

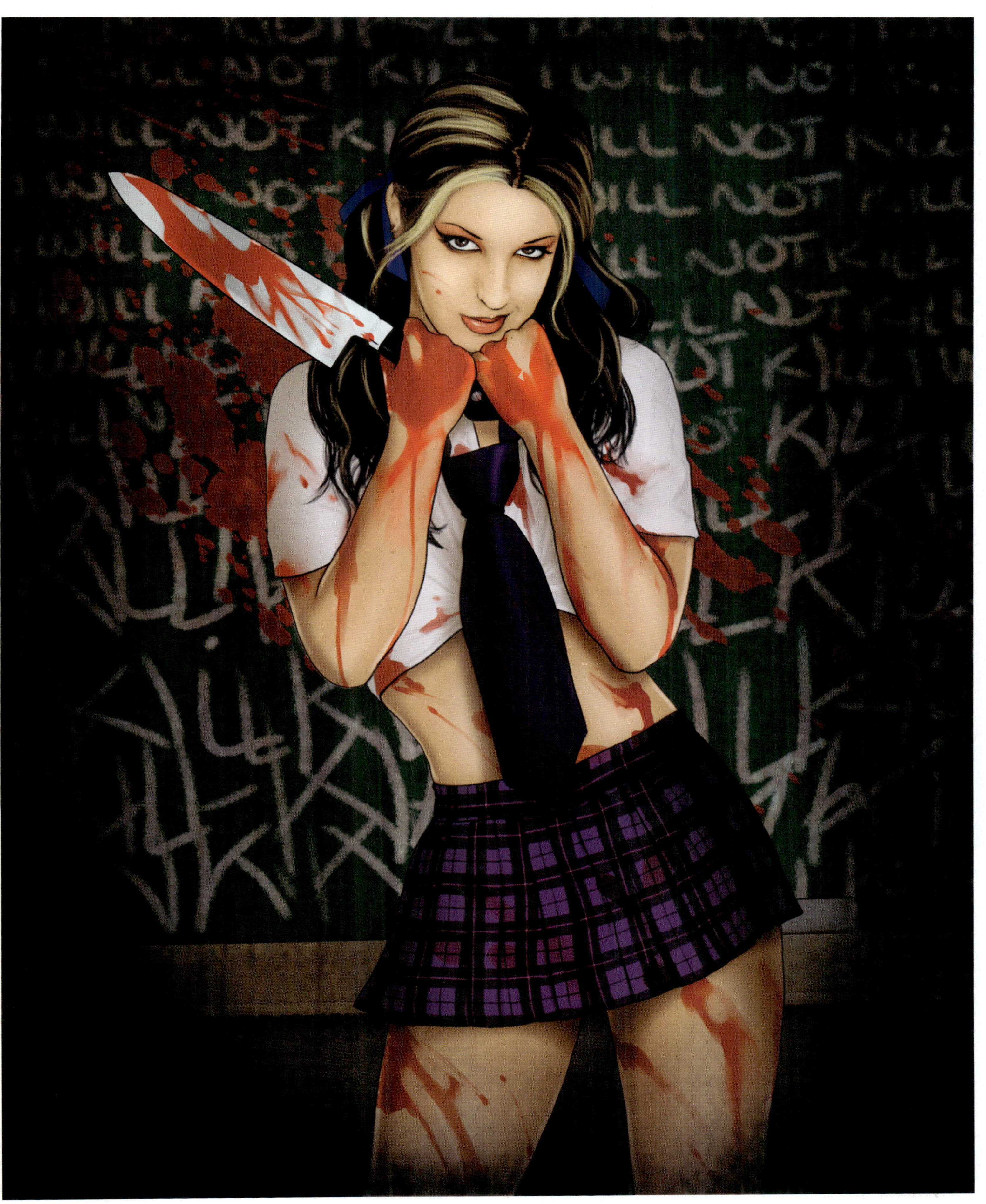
WILL NOT KILL

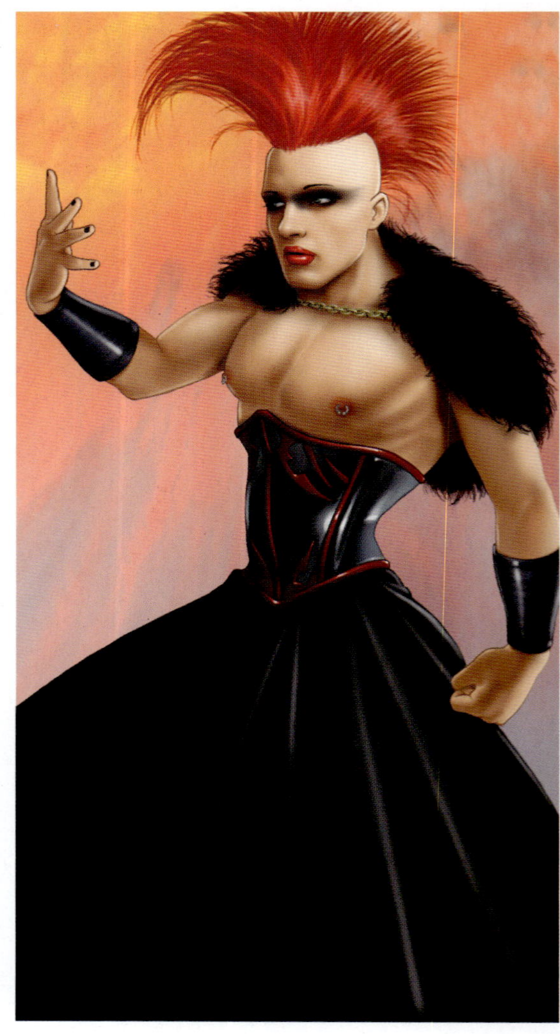

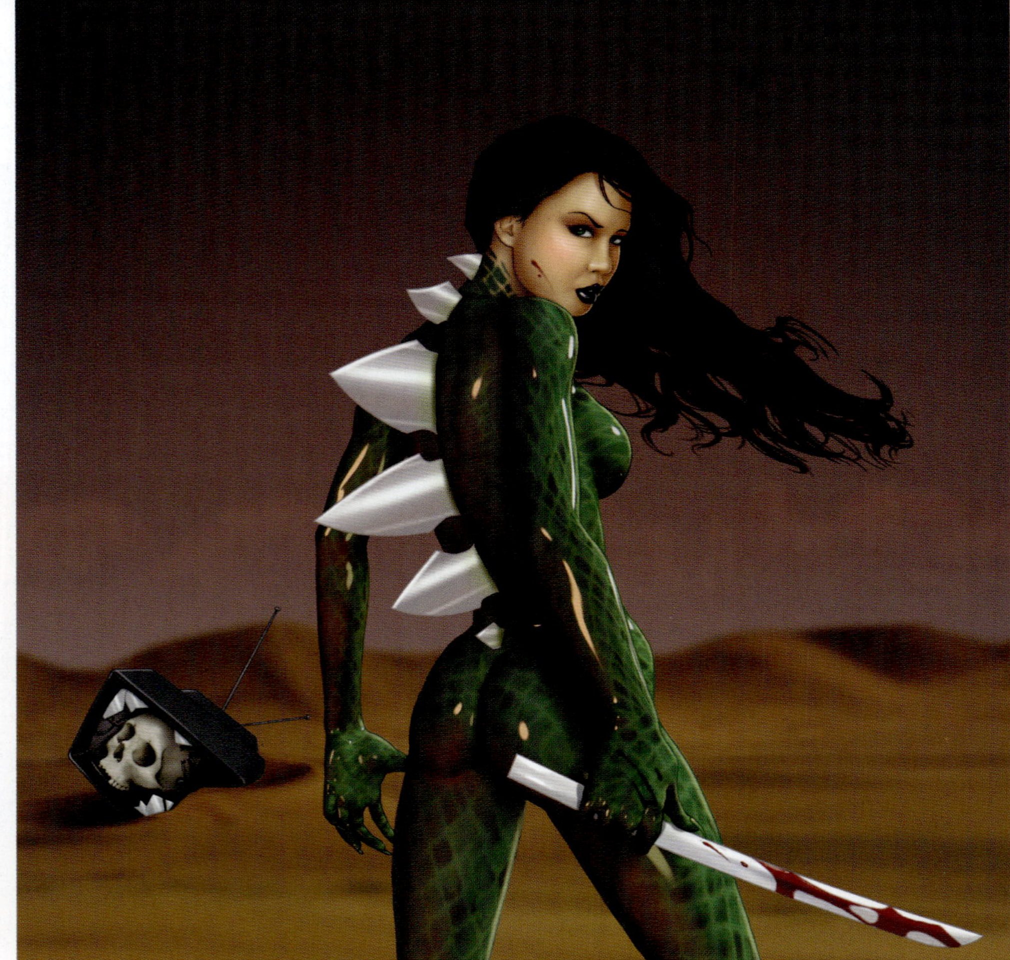

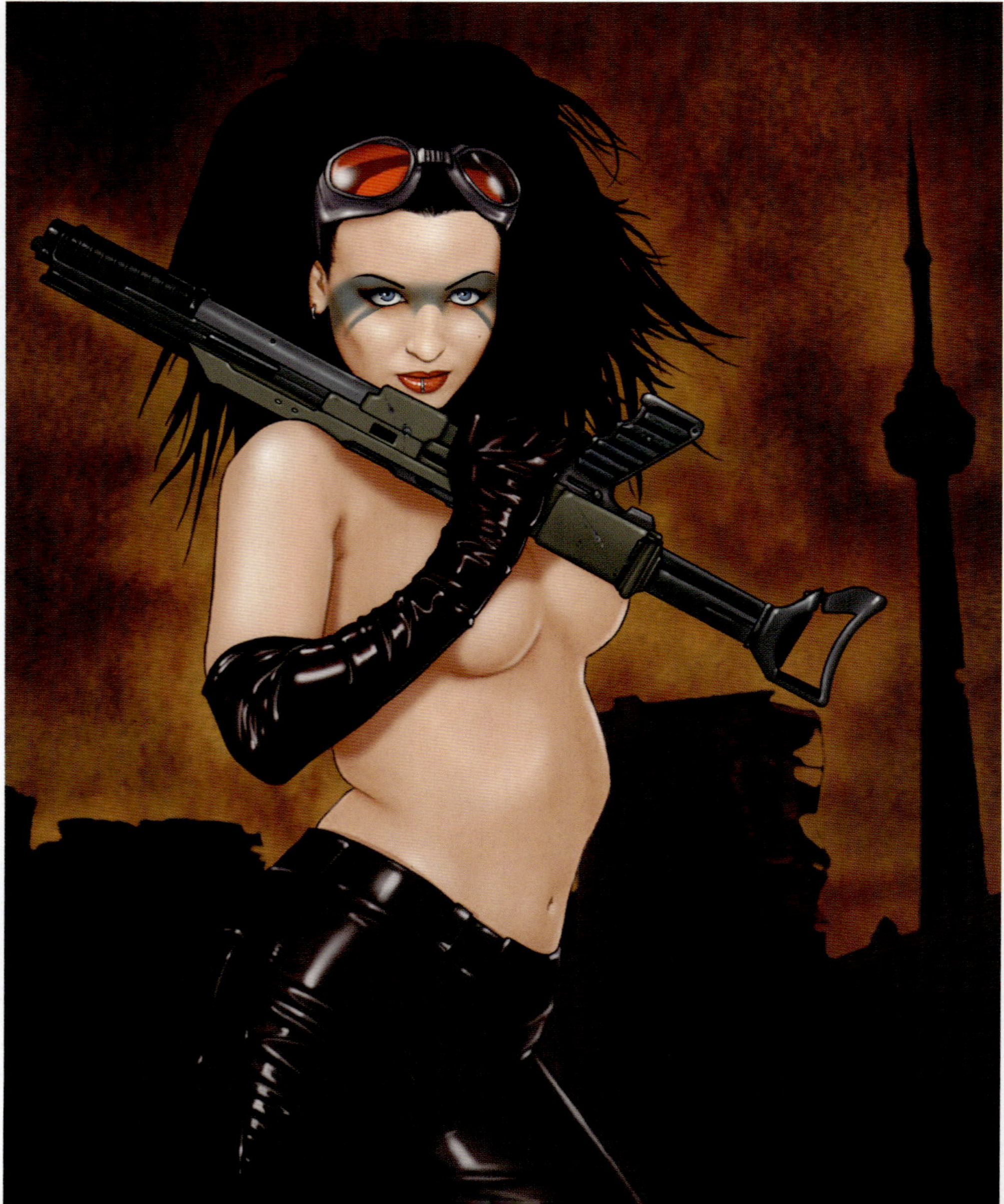

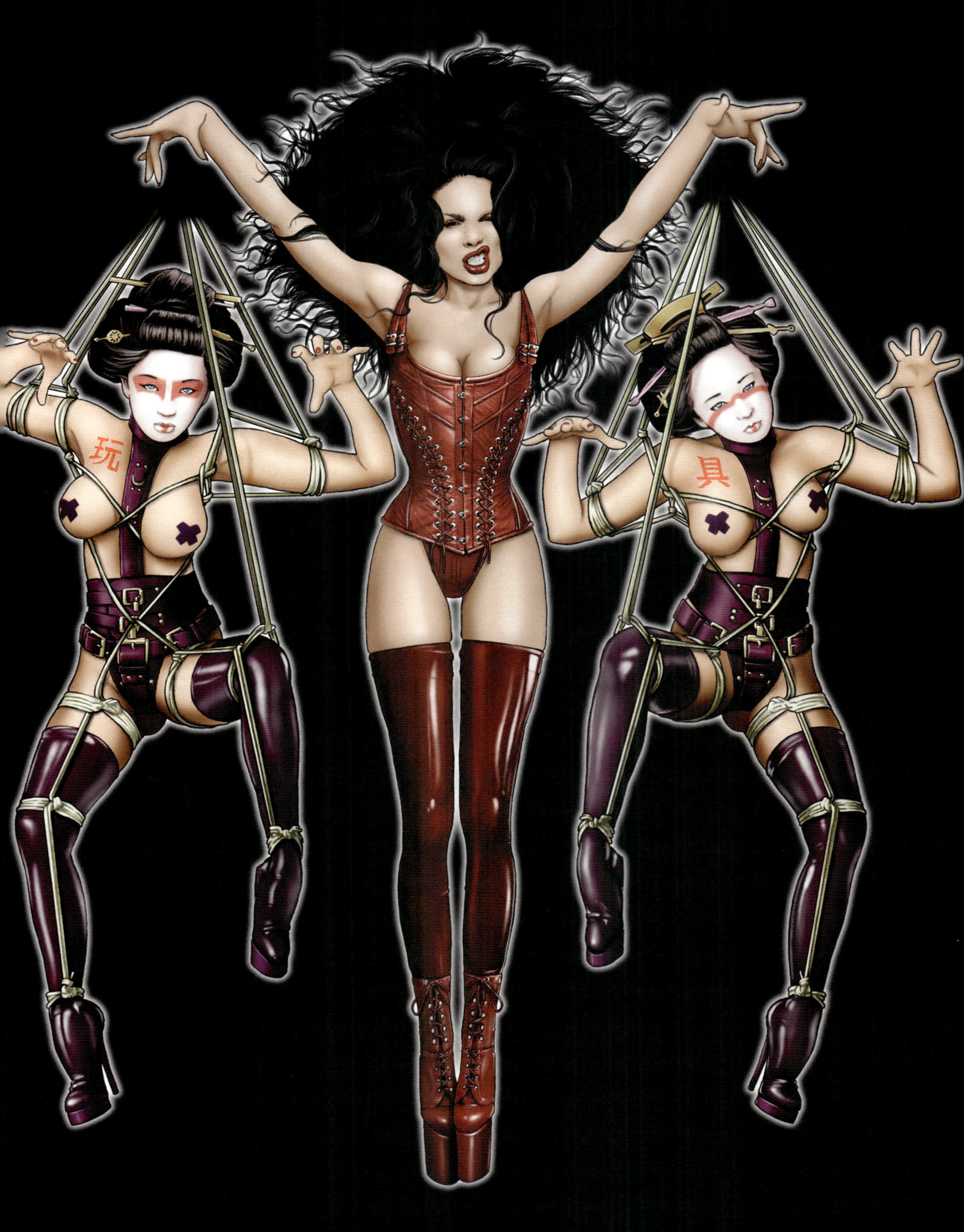
玩
具

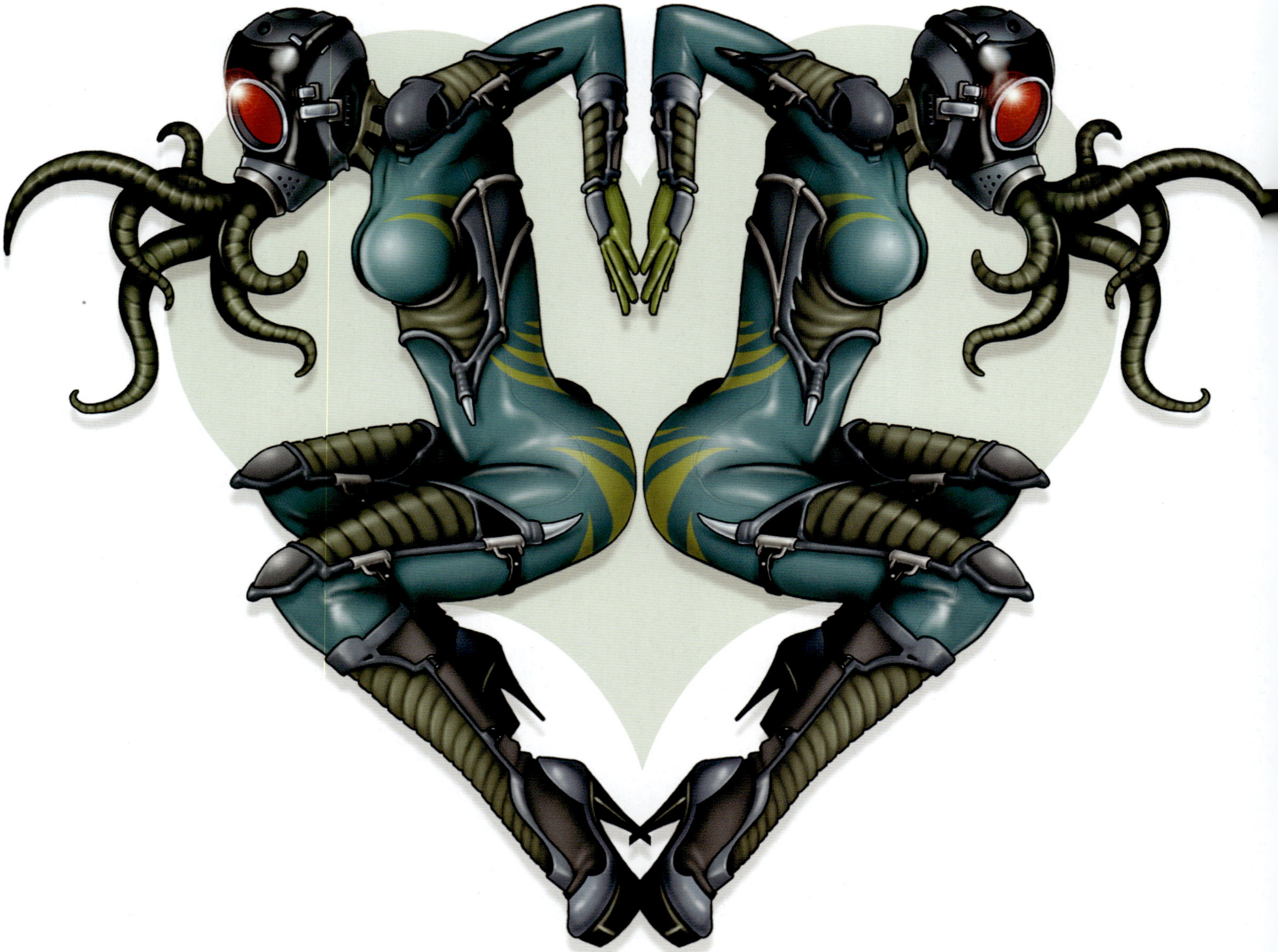

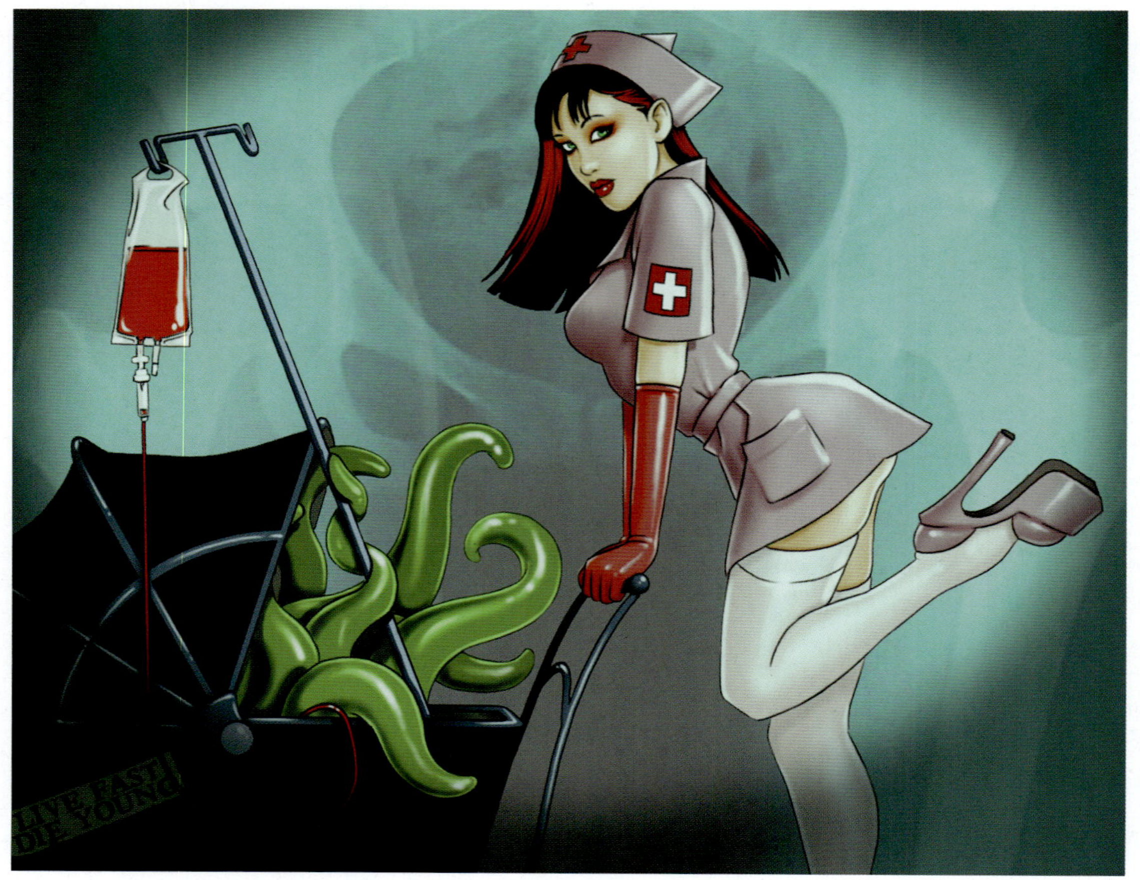
LIVE FAST
DIE YOUNG

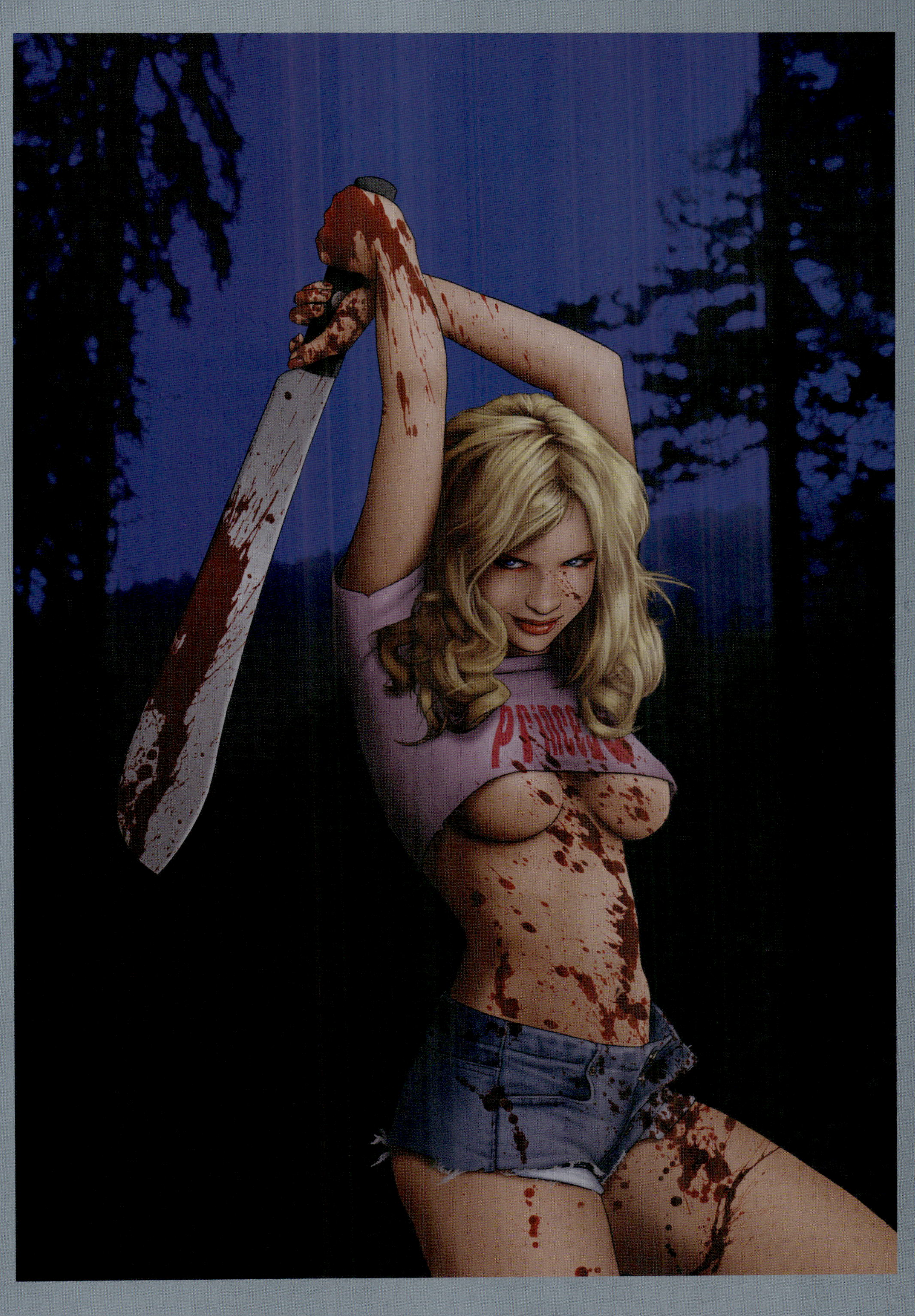

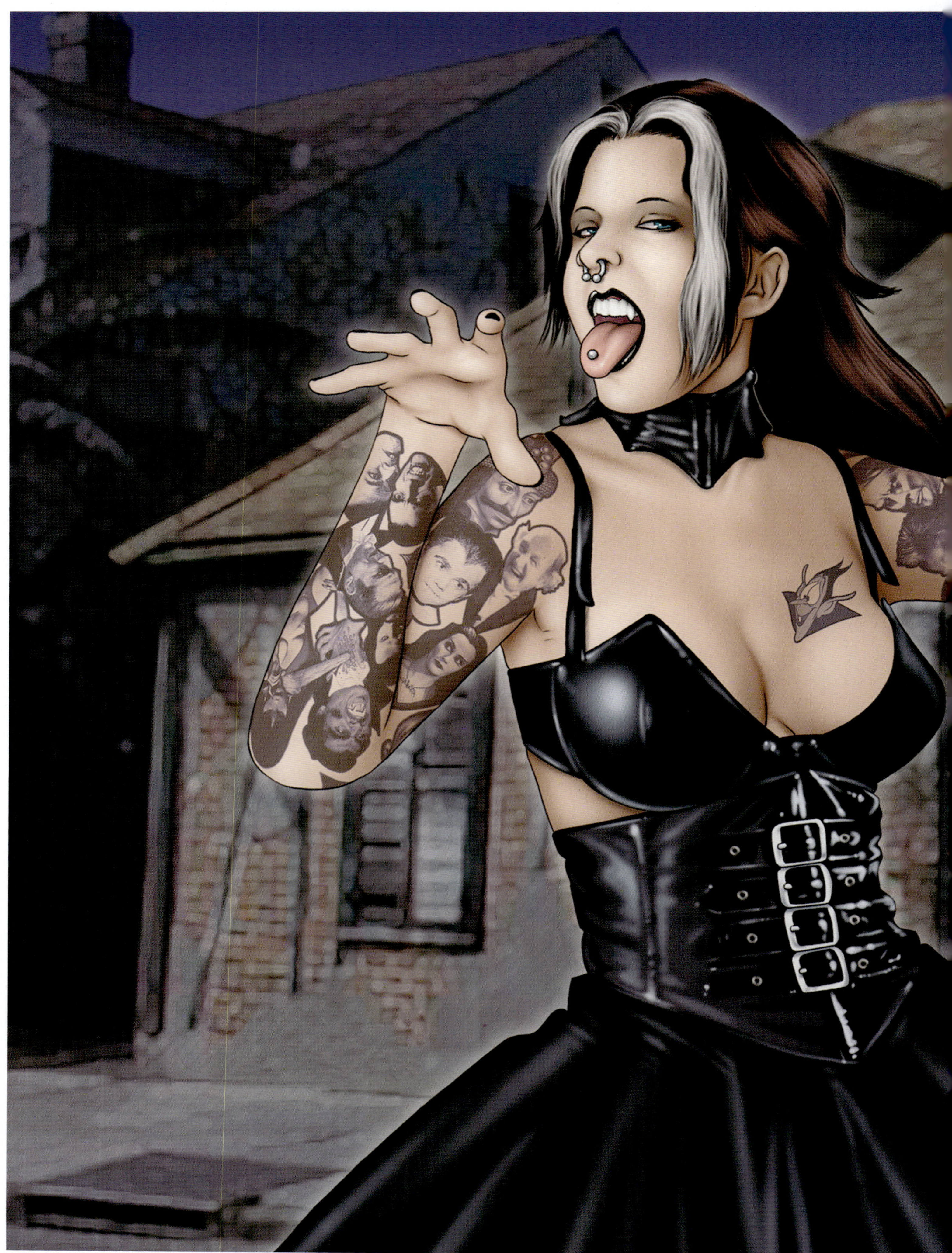

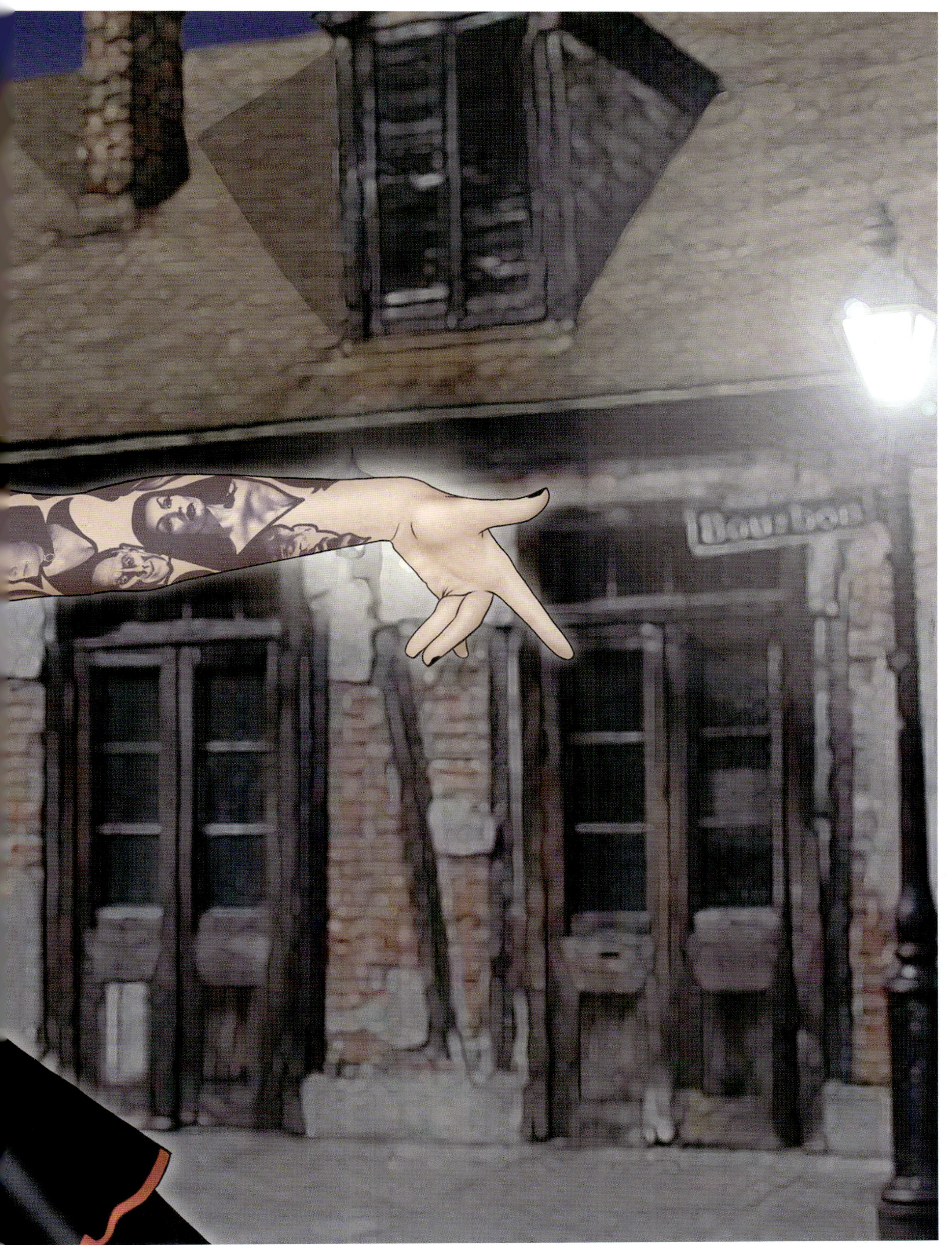
Bourbon

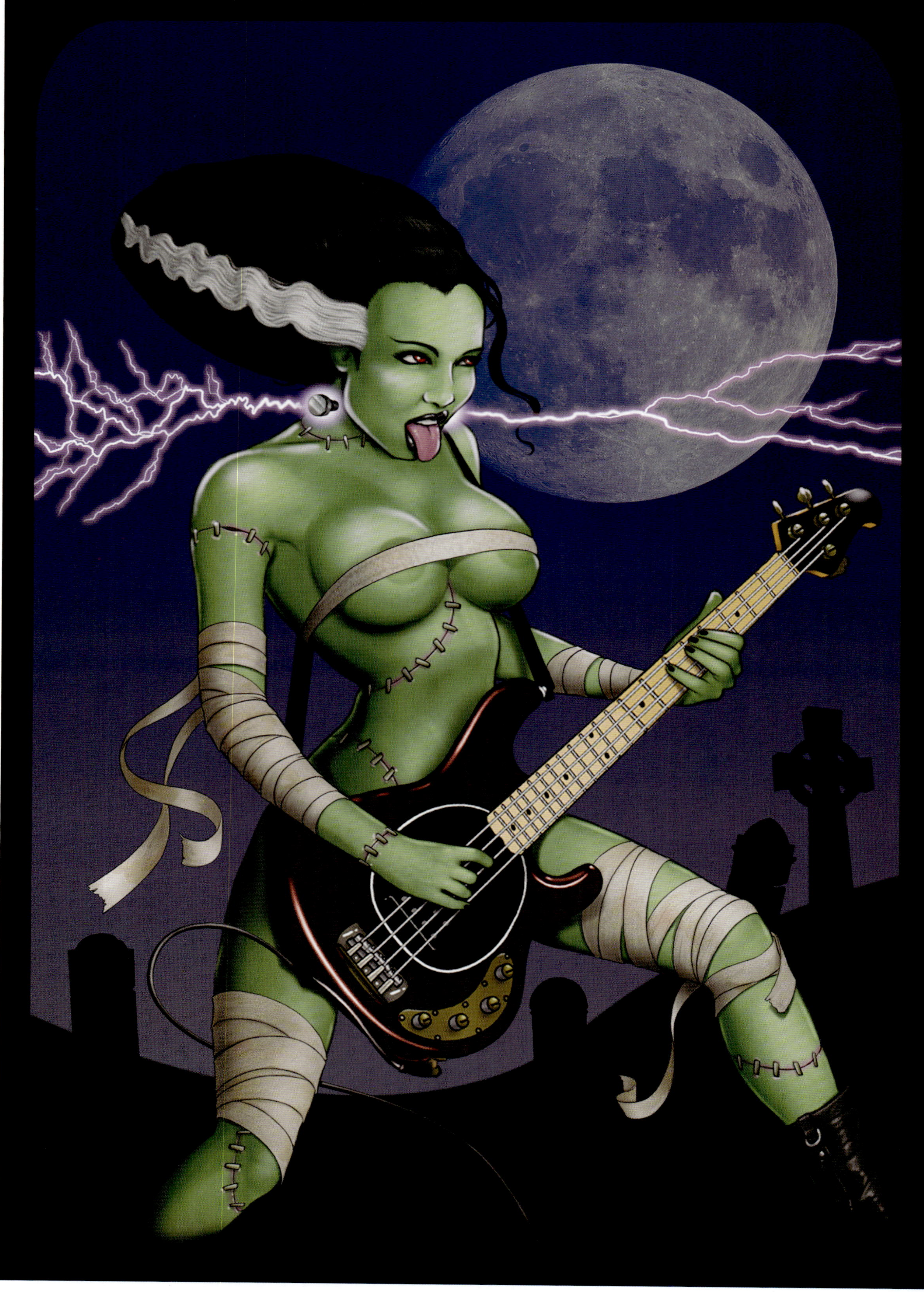

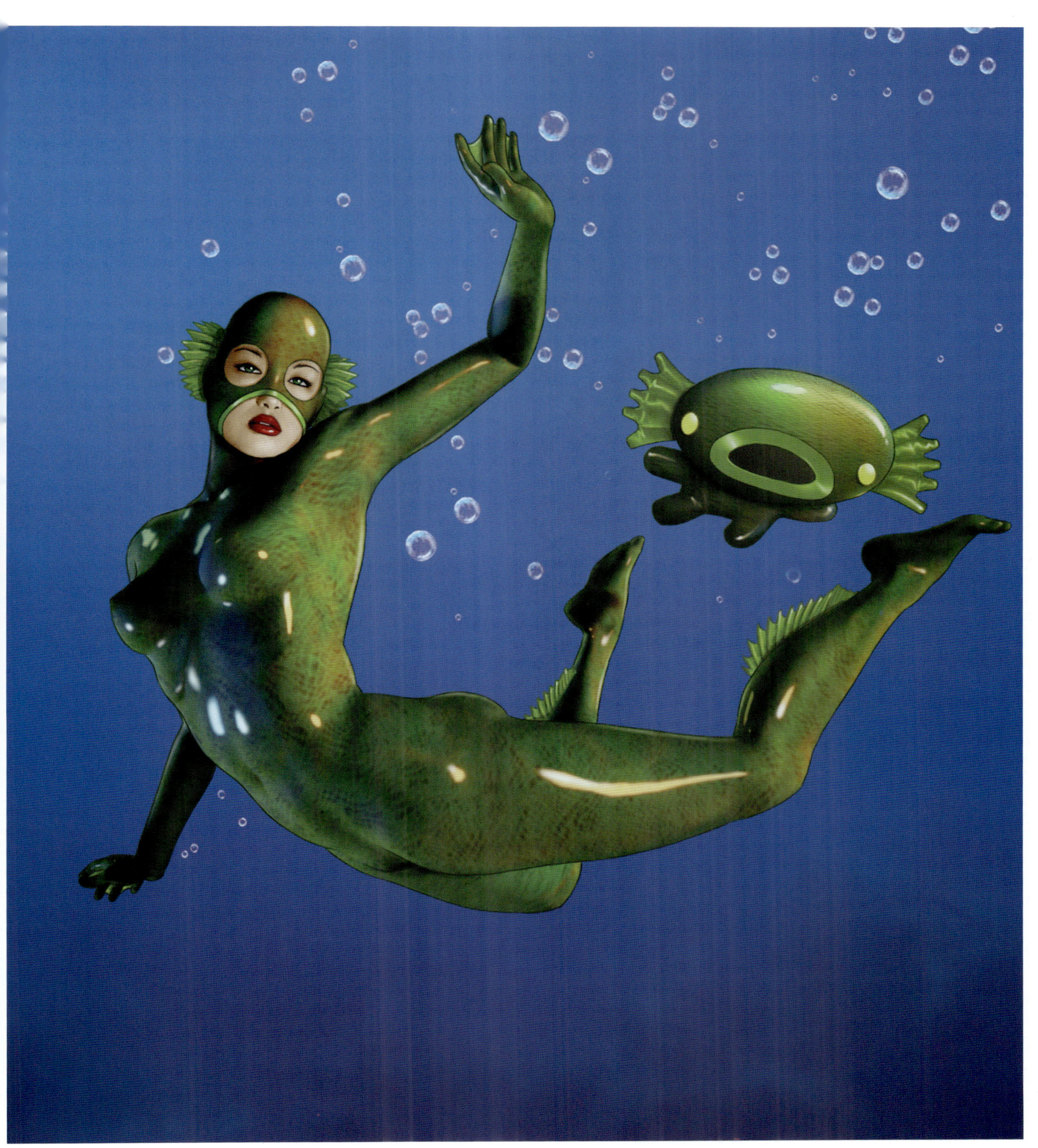

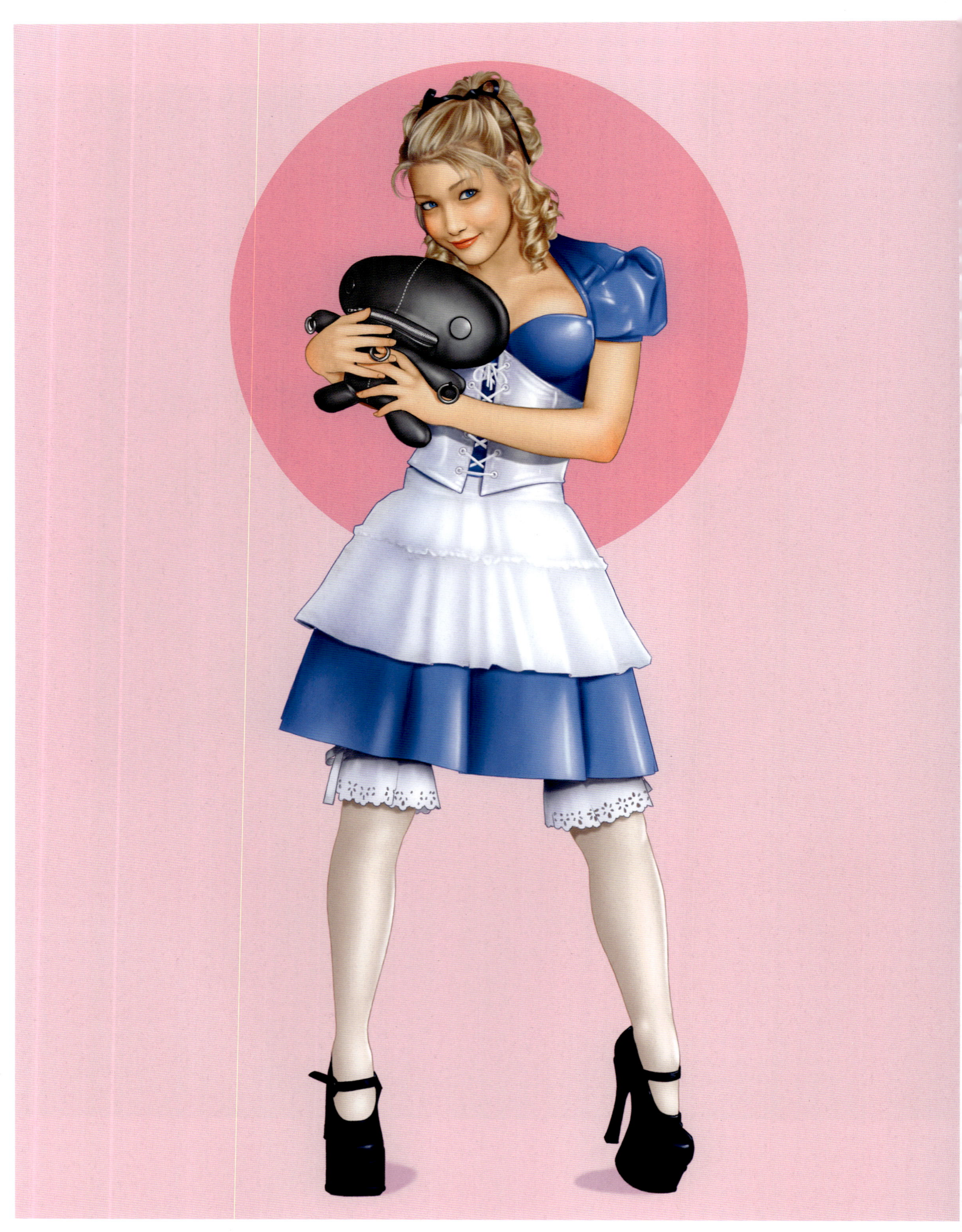

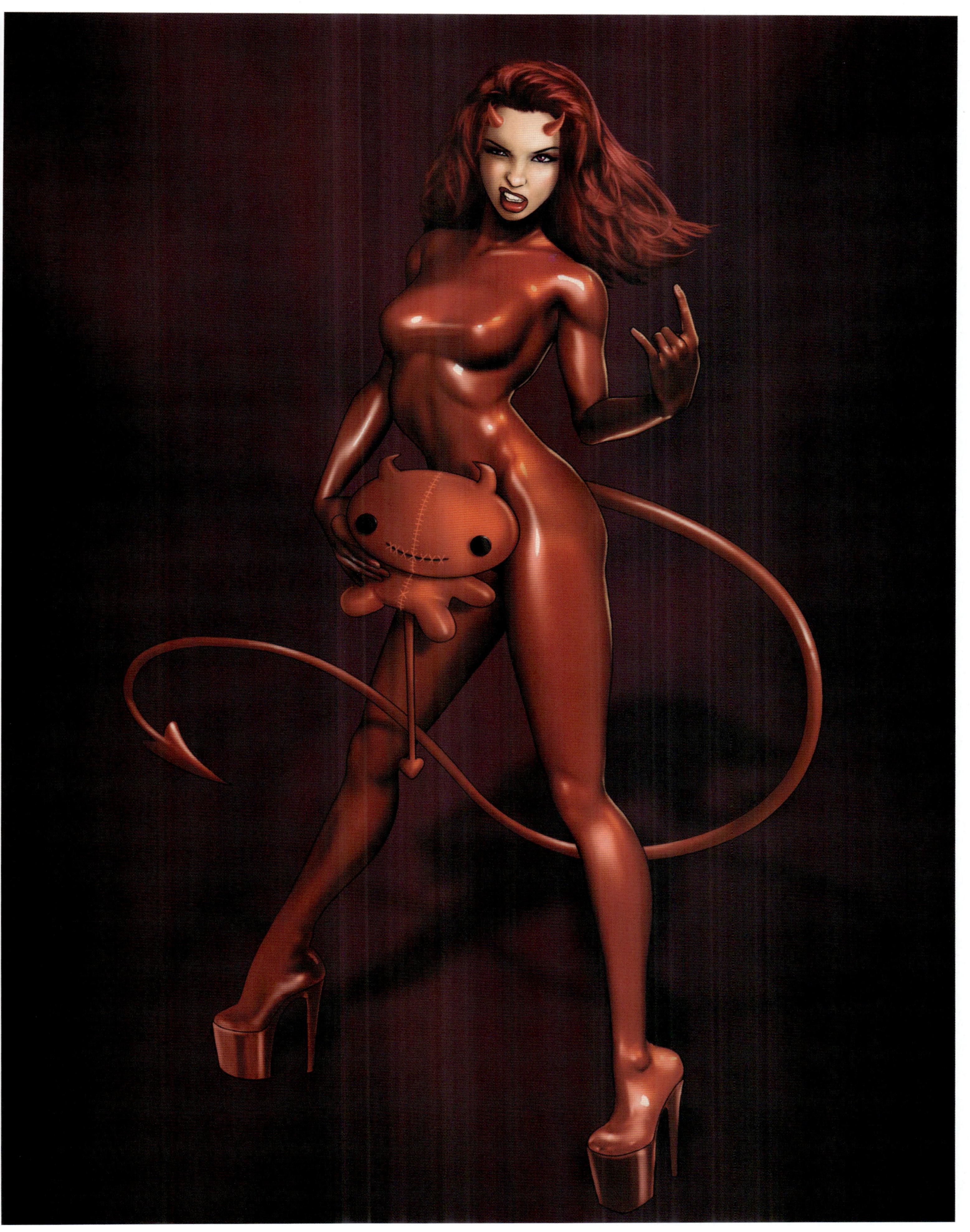

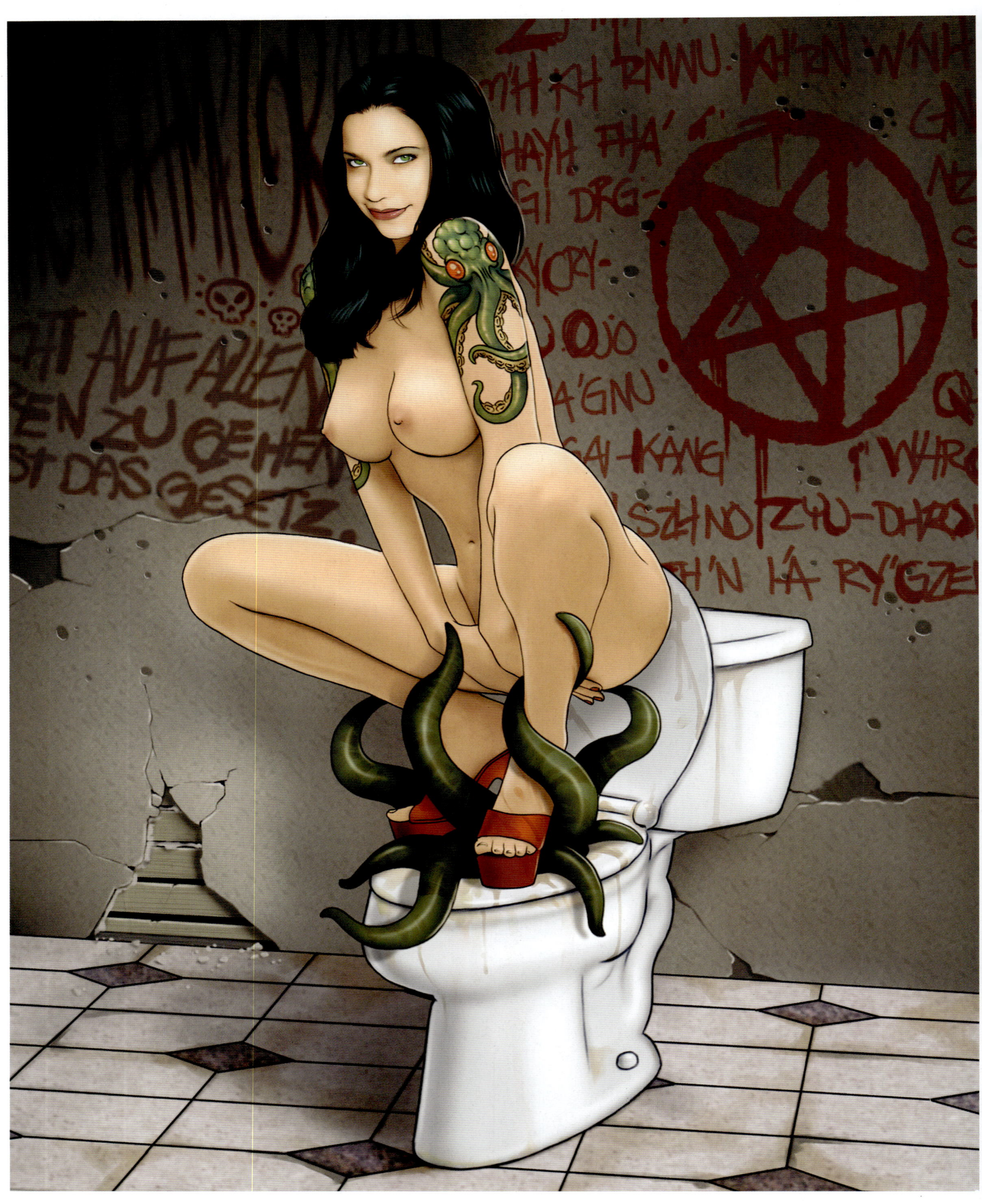
AUF ALLEN
EN ZU GEHEN
ST DAS GESETZ
RMNU. KH'EN WNH
HAYH FHA'
GI DRG-
KY'CRY-
A'GNU
GAI-KANG
SZHNO ZYU-DHRO

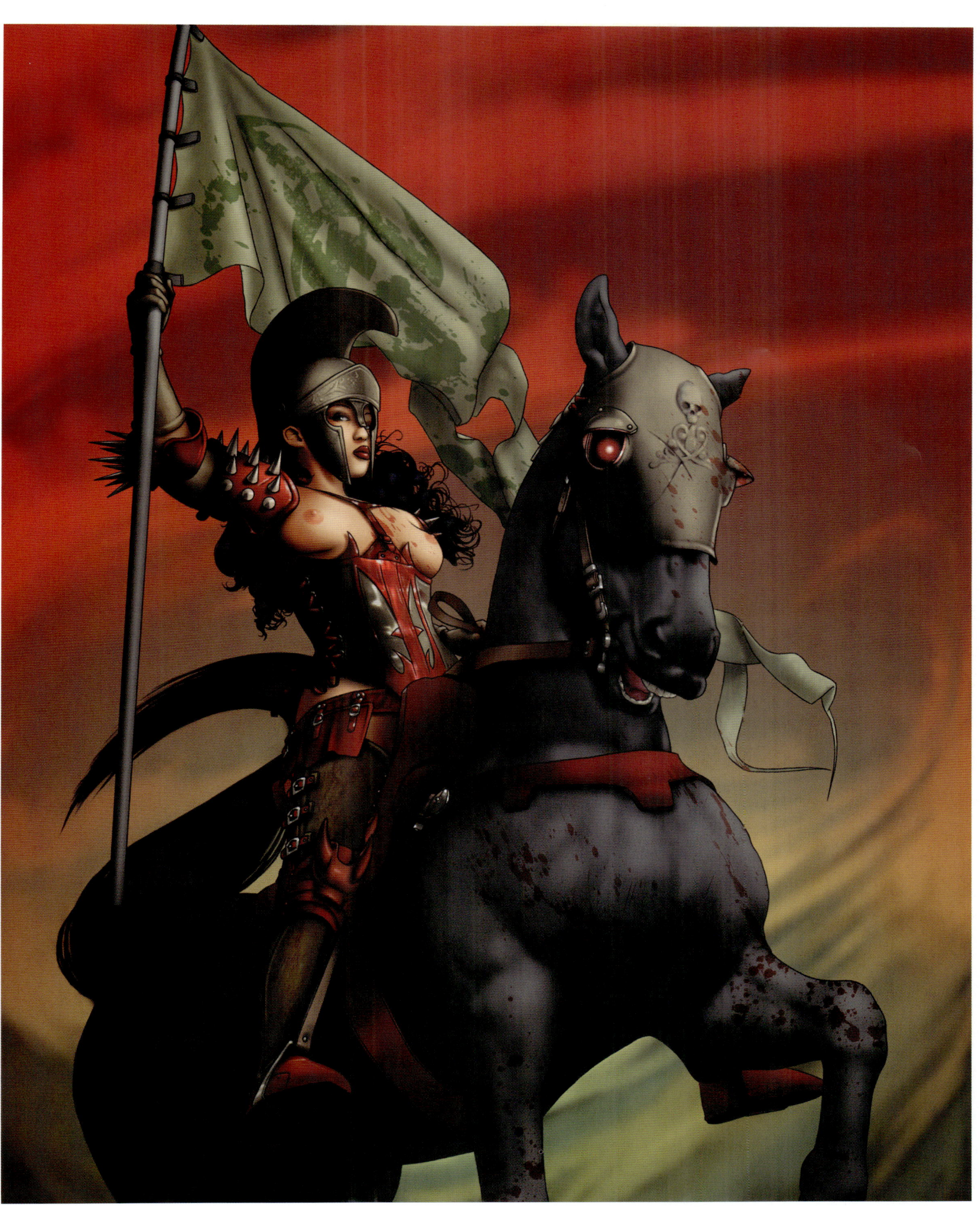

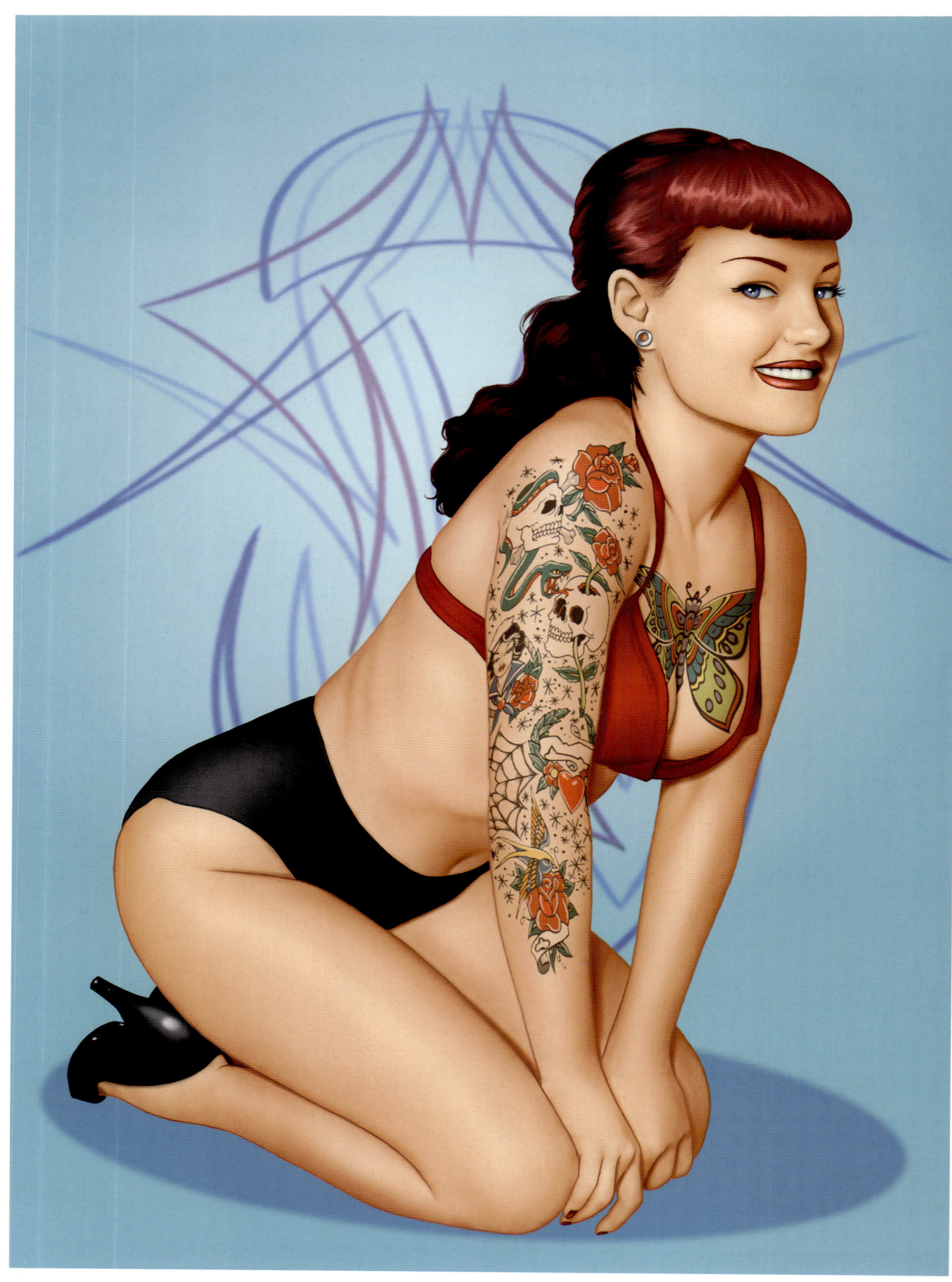

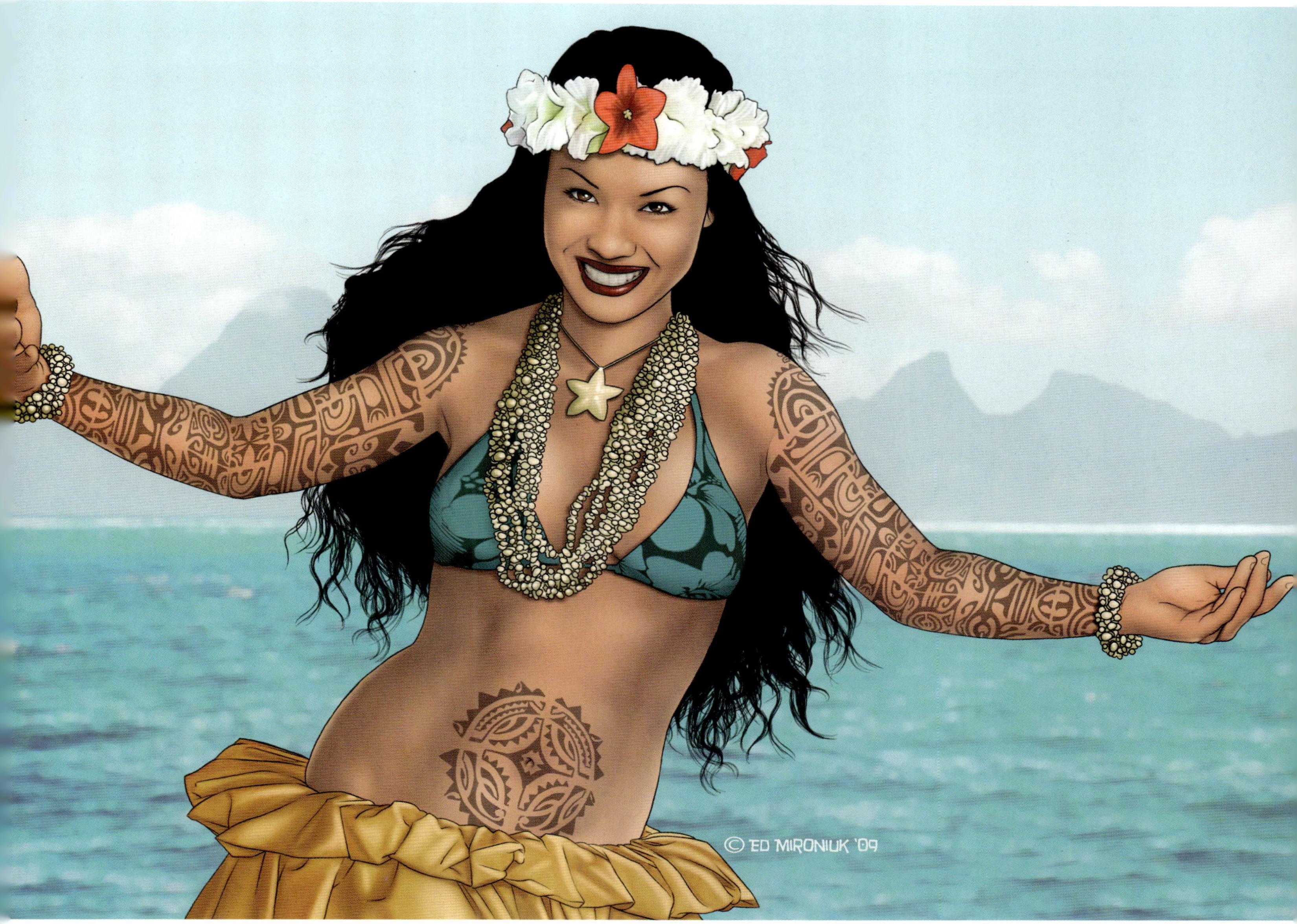

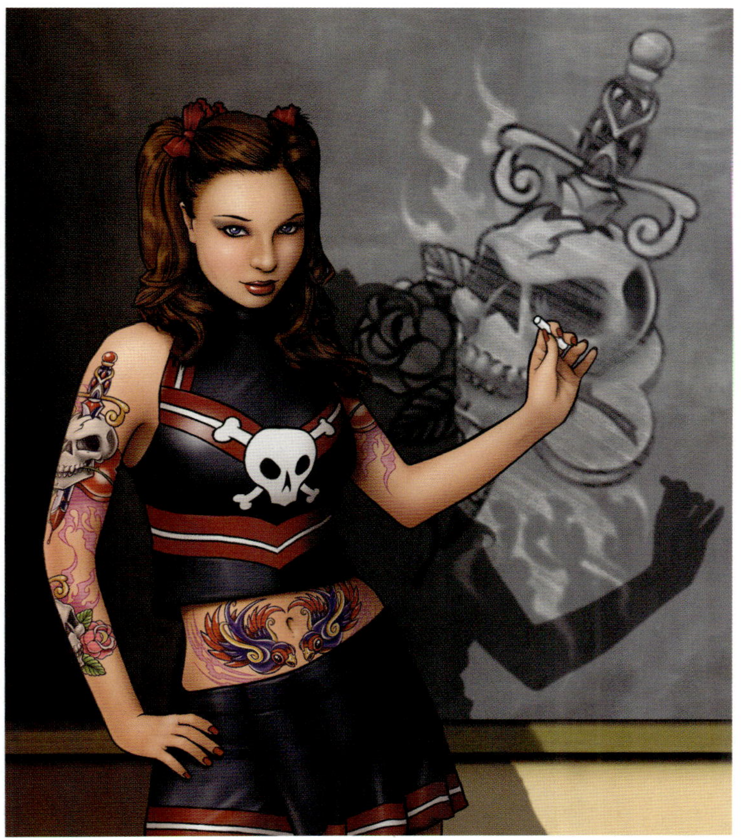

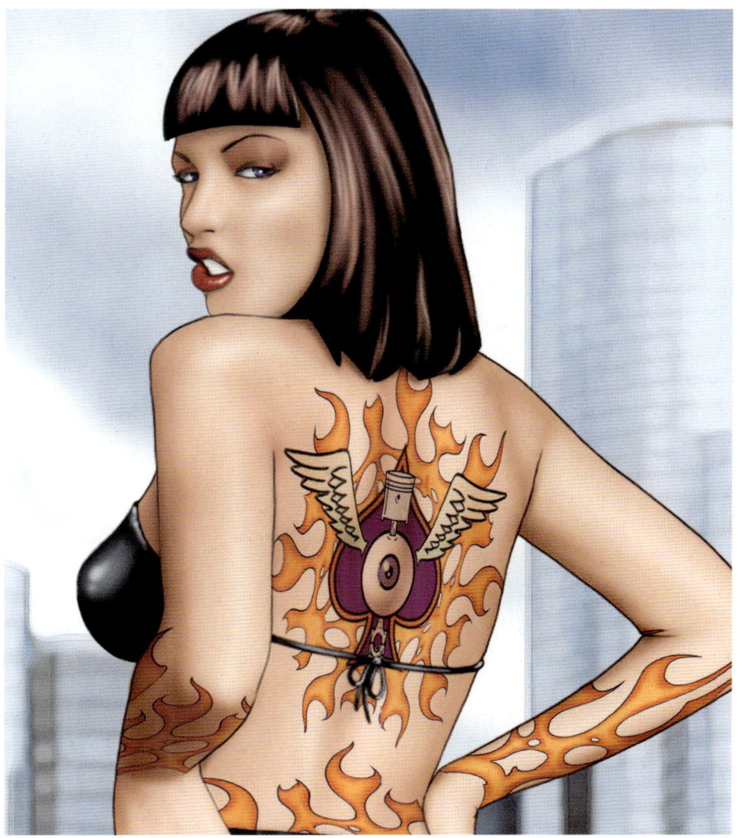

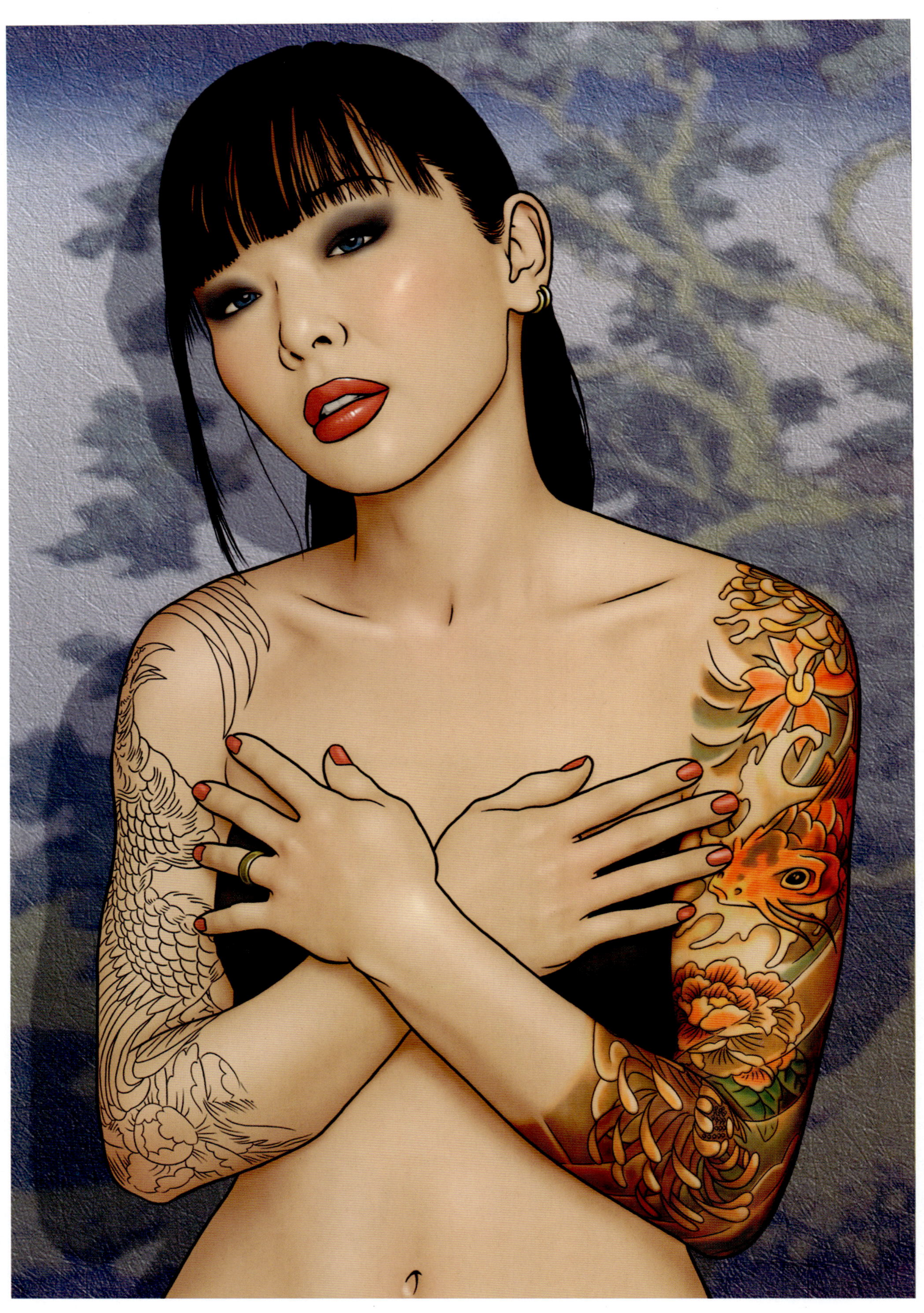

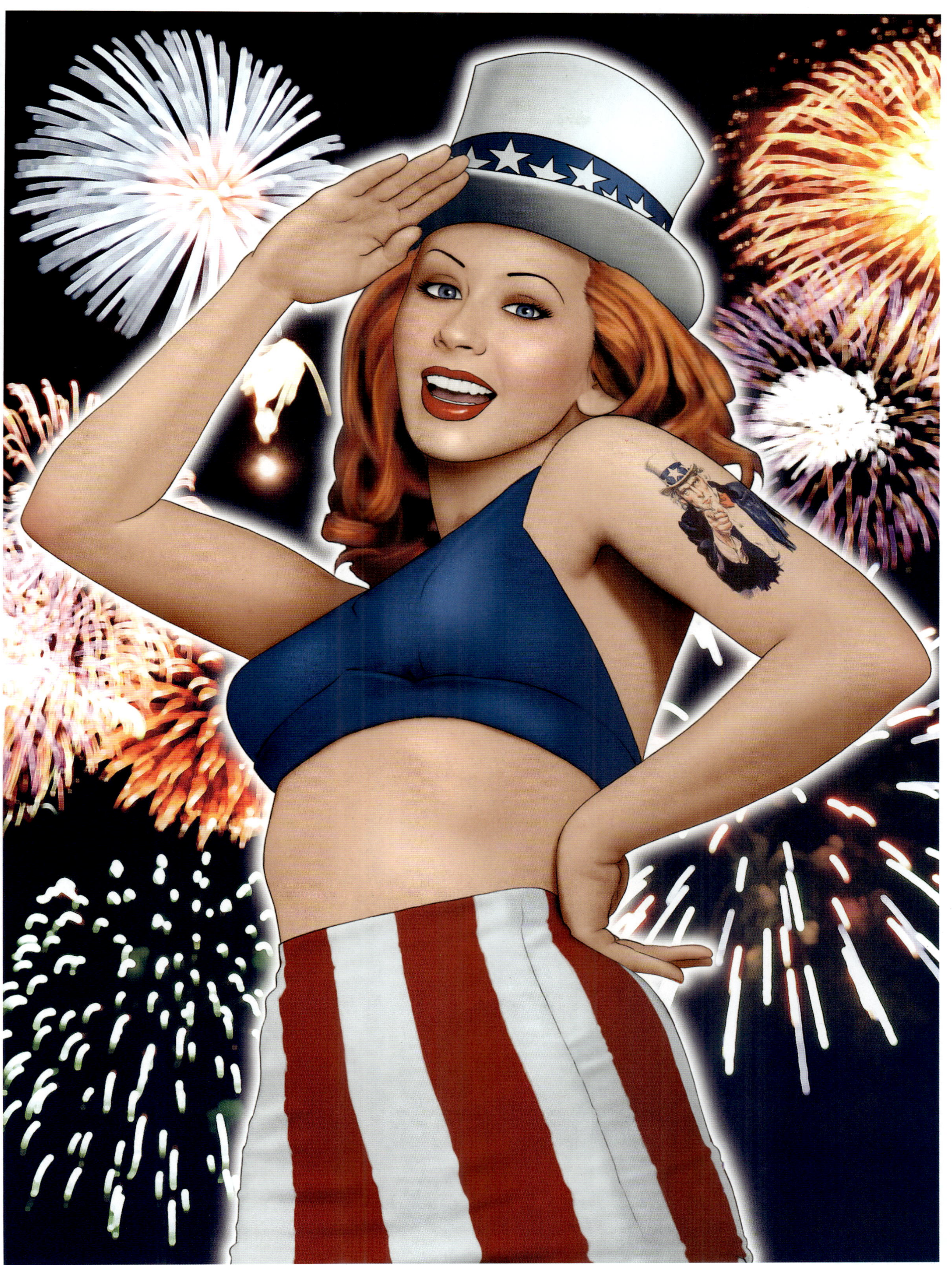

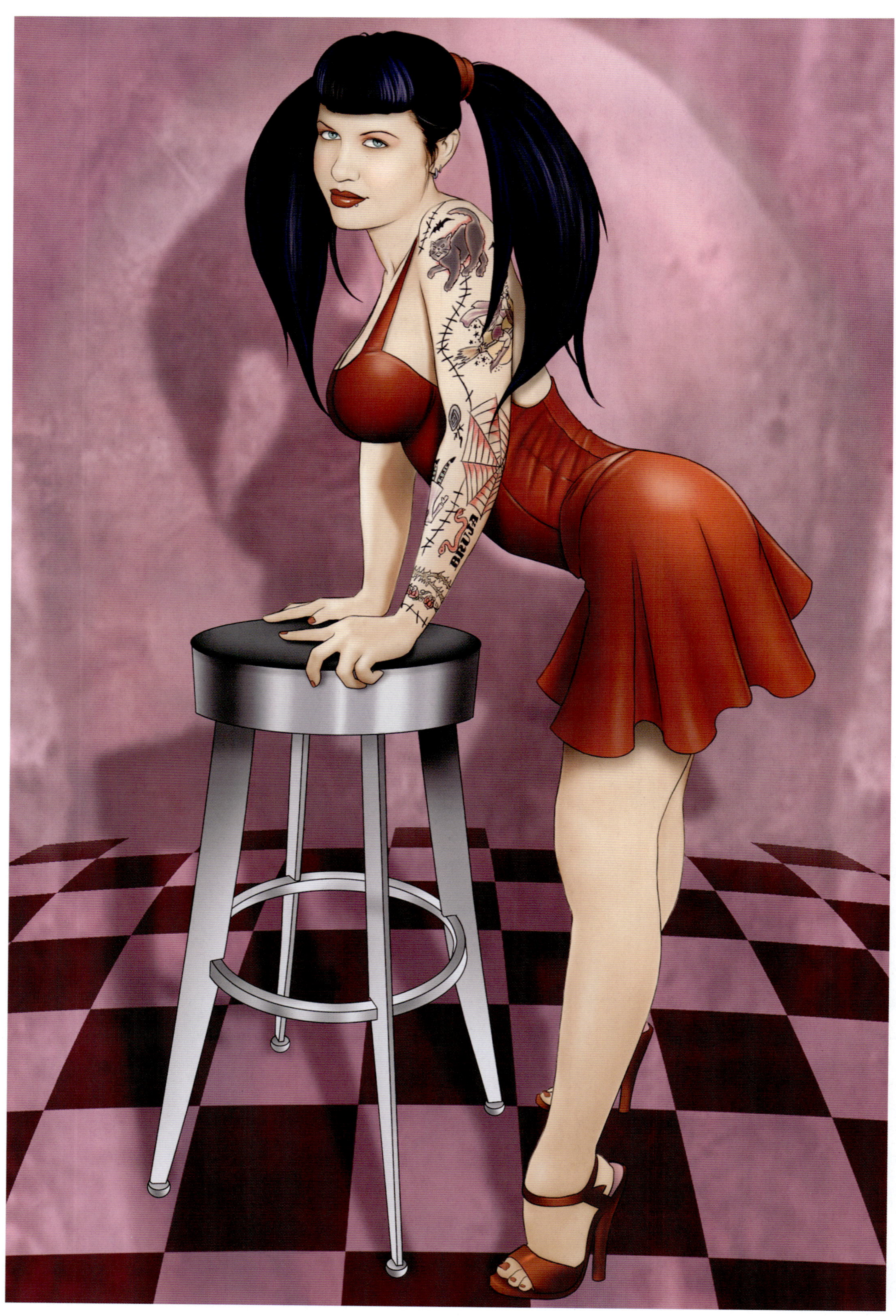
BRUJA

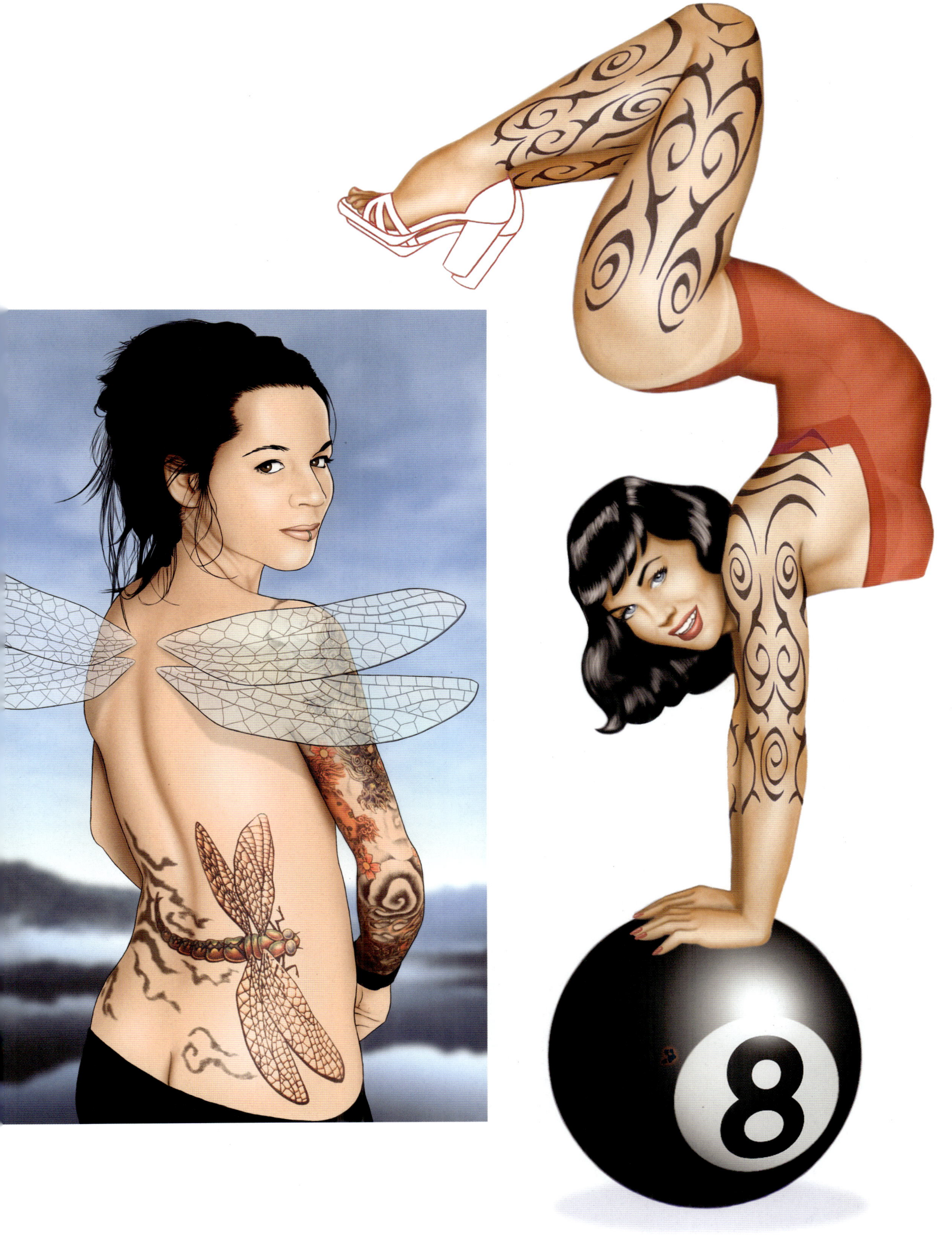

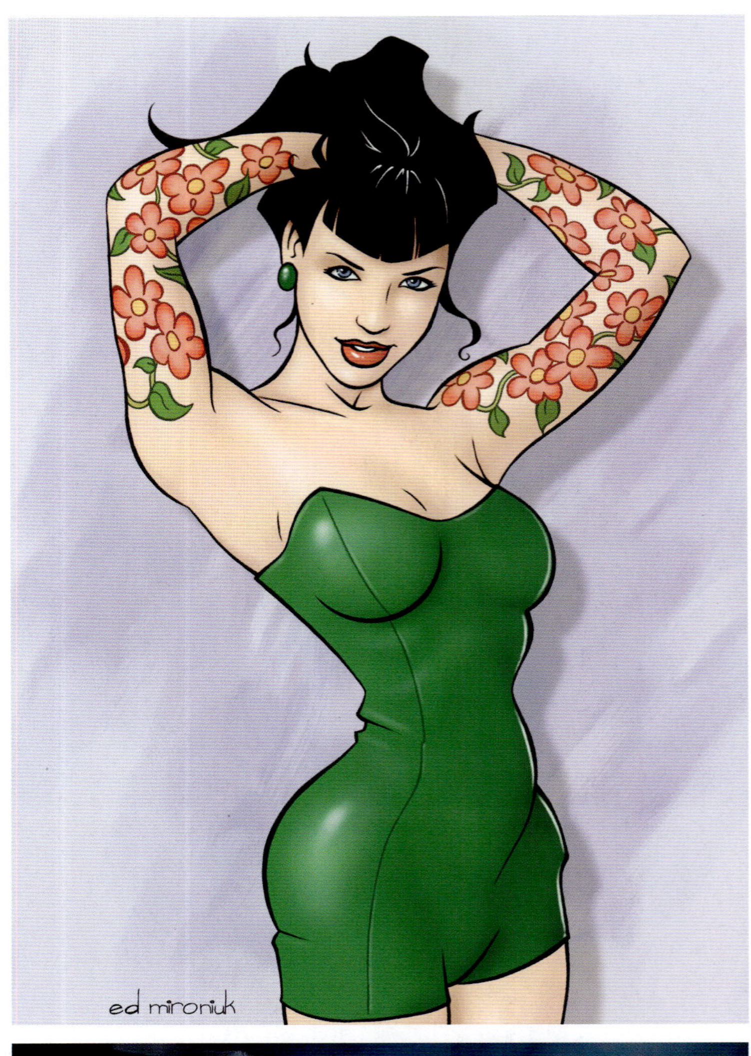
ed mironiuk

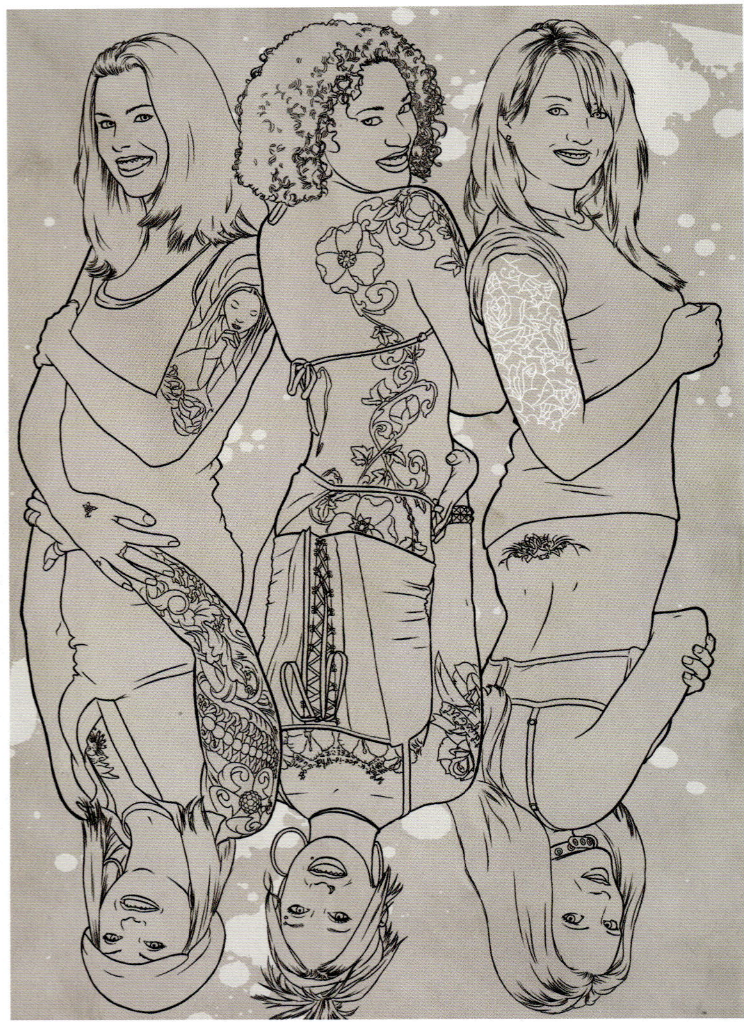

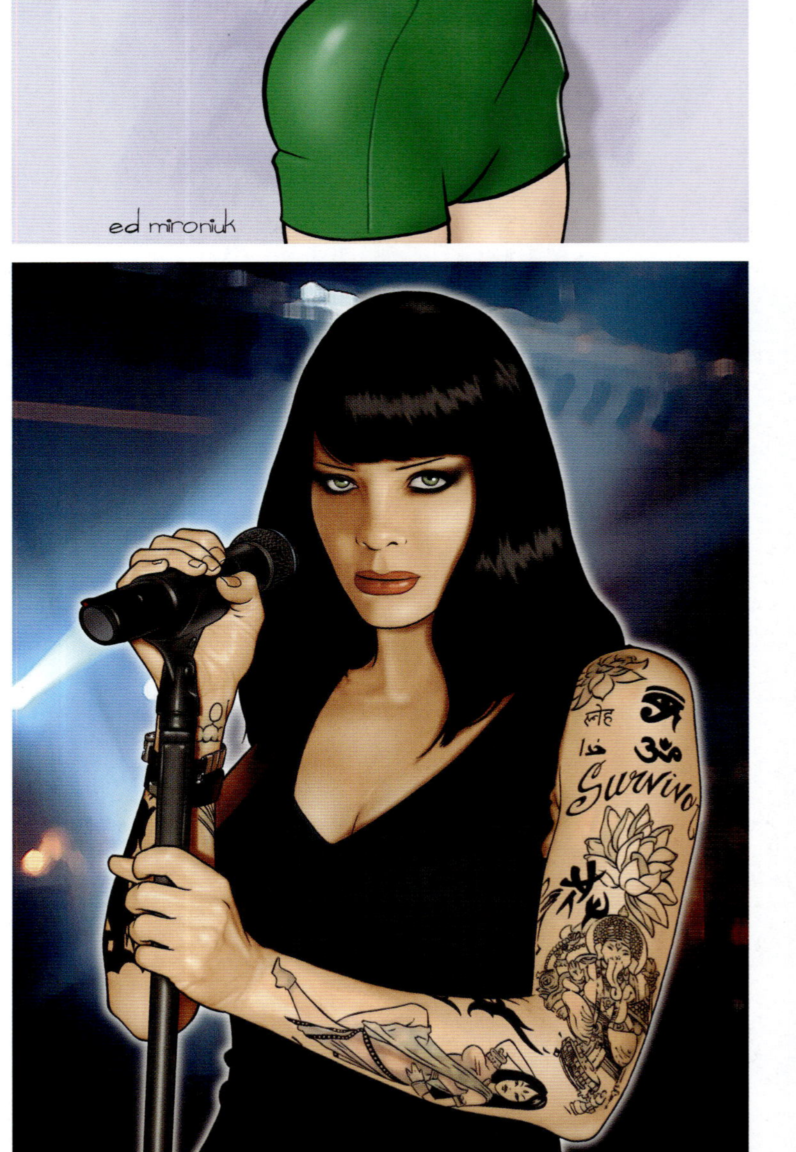

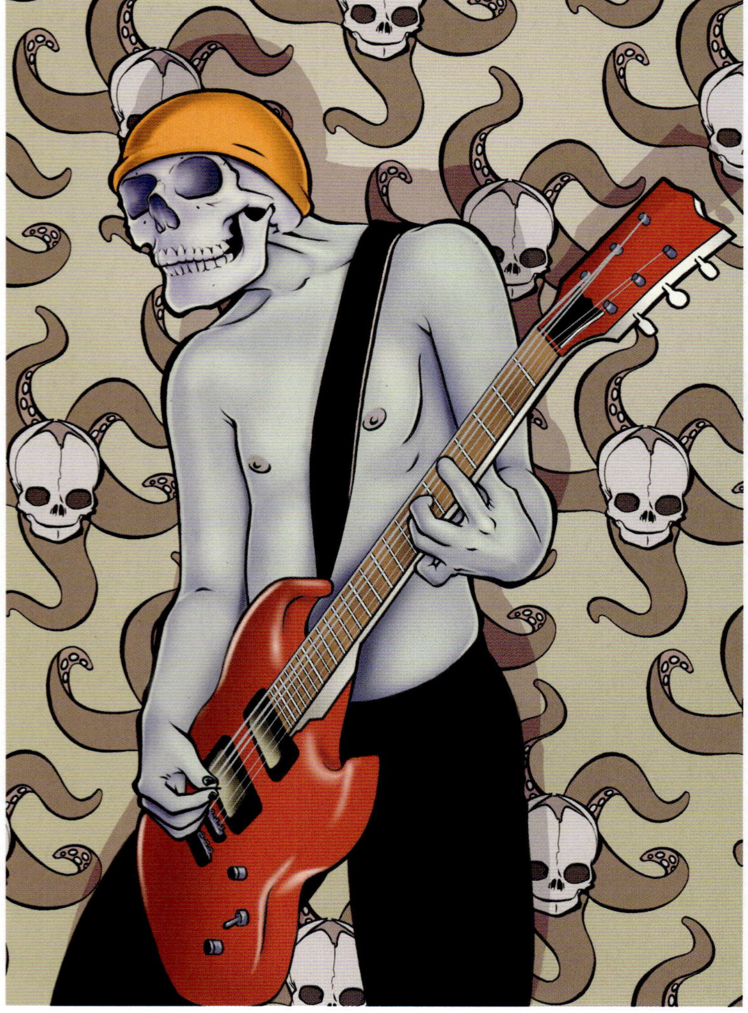

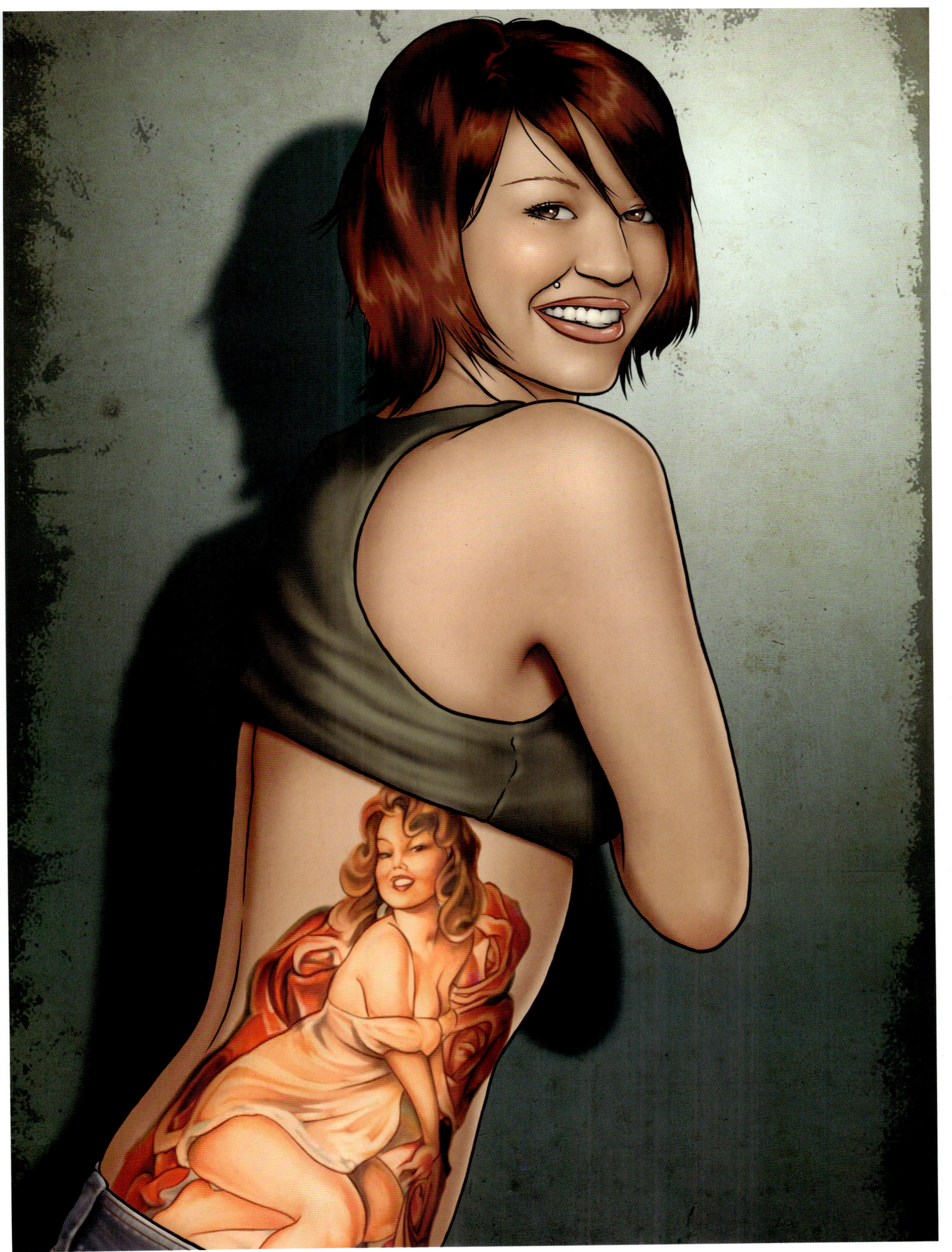

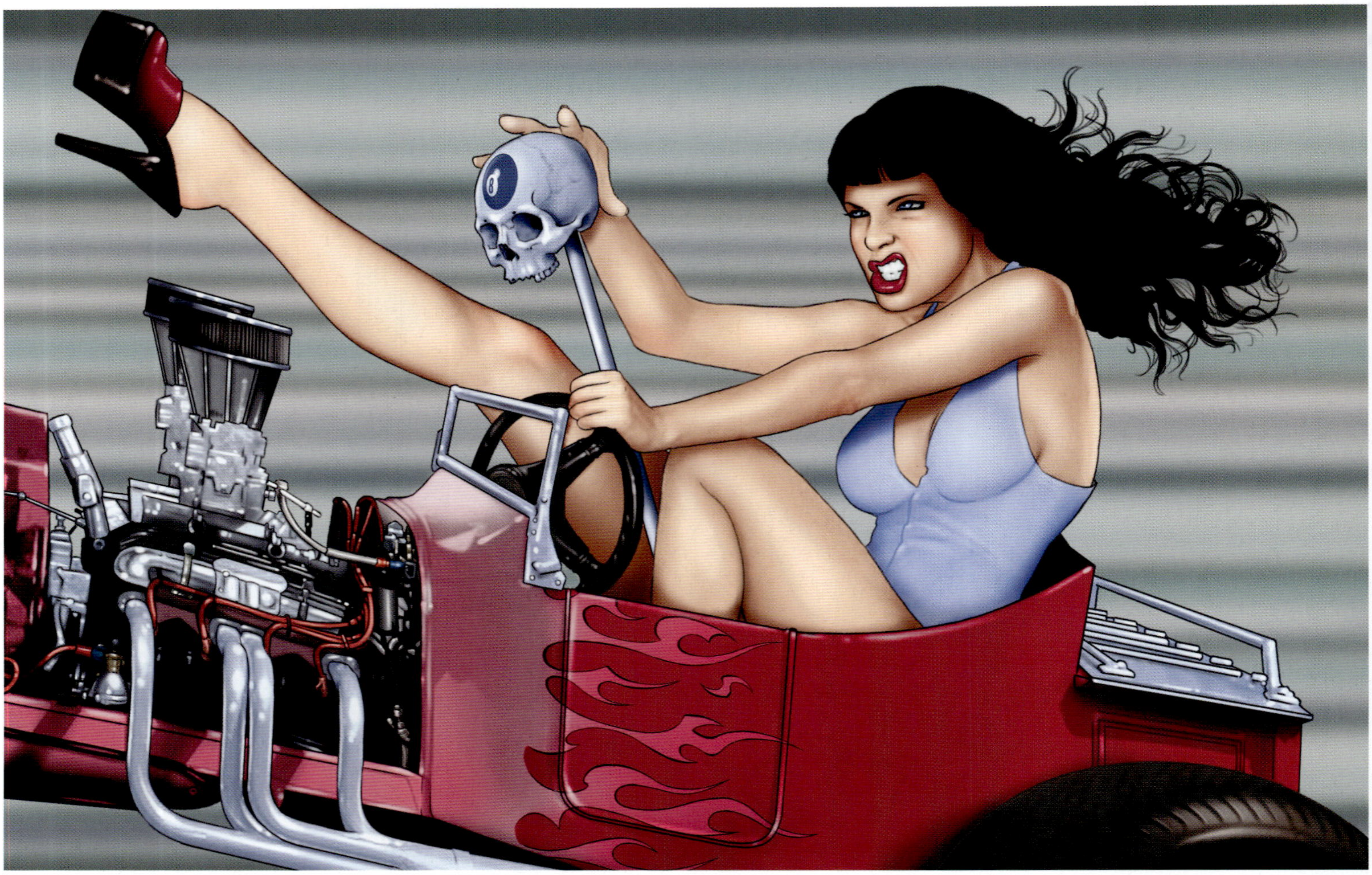

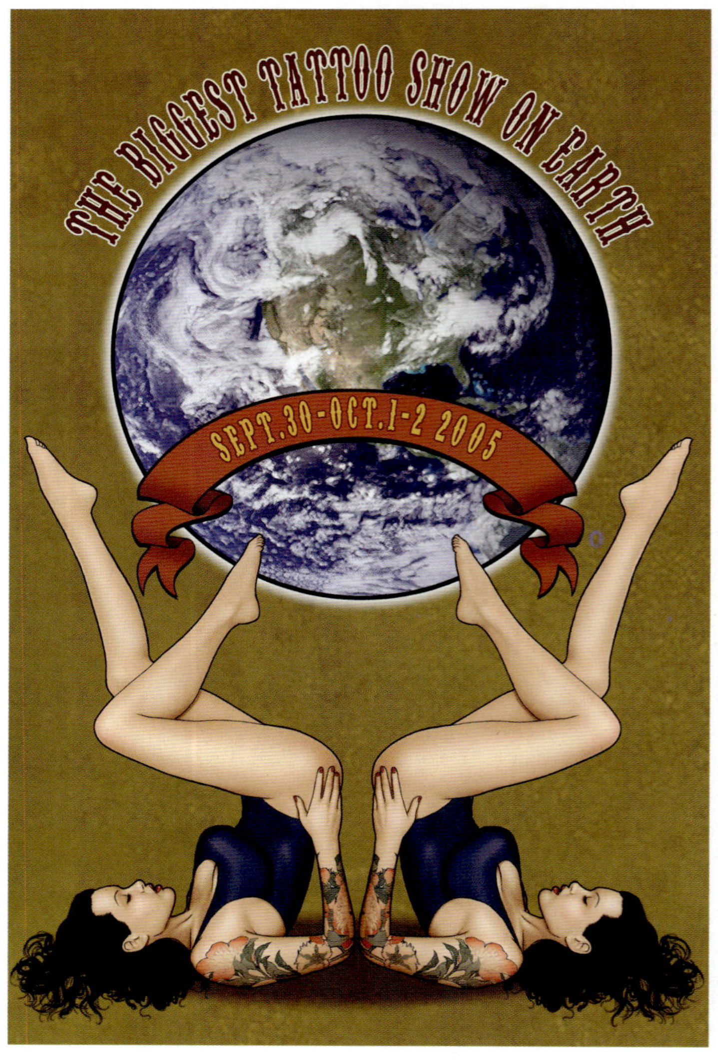
THE BIGGEST TATTOO SHOW ON EARTH
SEPT.30-OCT.1-2 2005

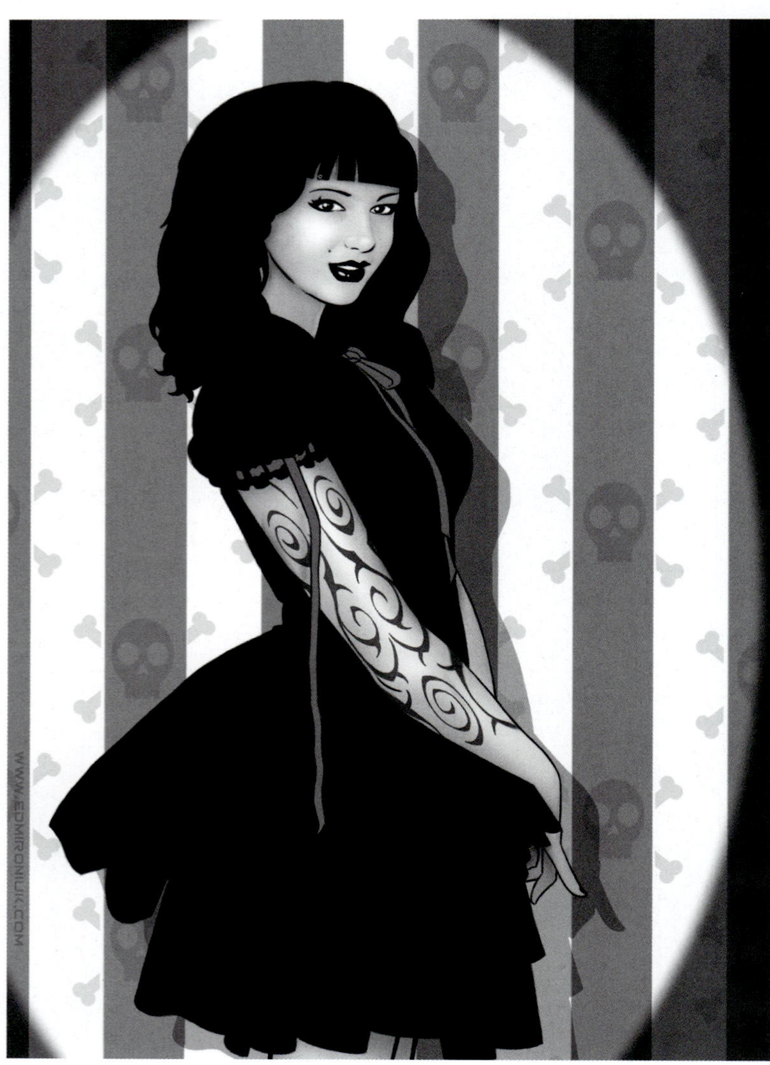
WWW.EDMIRONIUK.COM

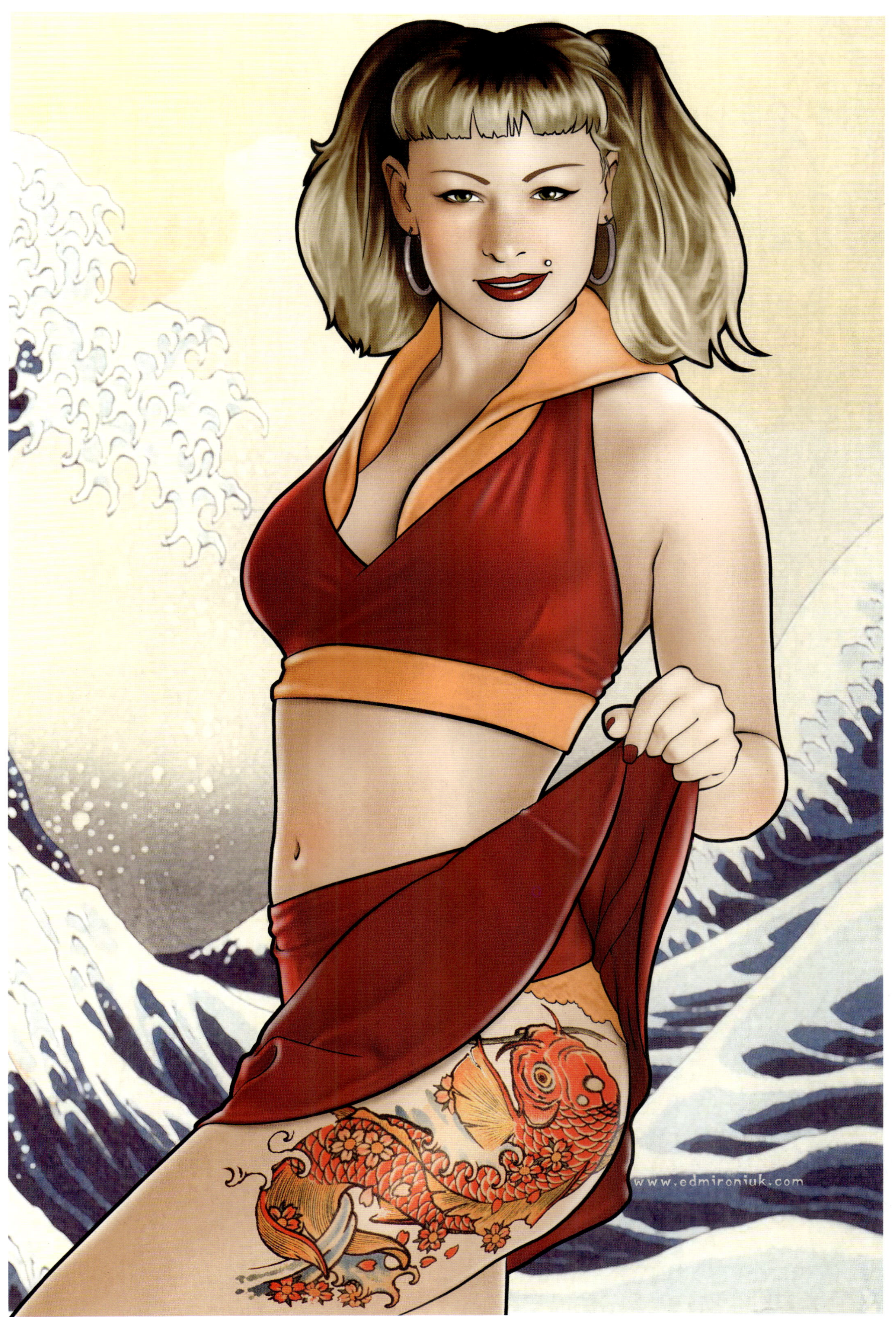
www.edmironiuk.com

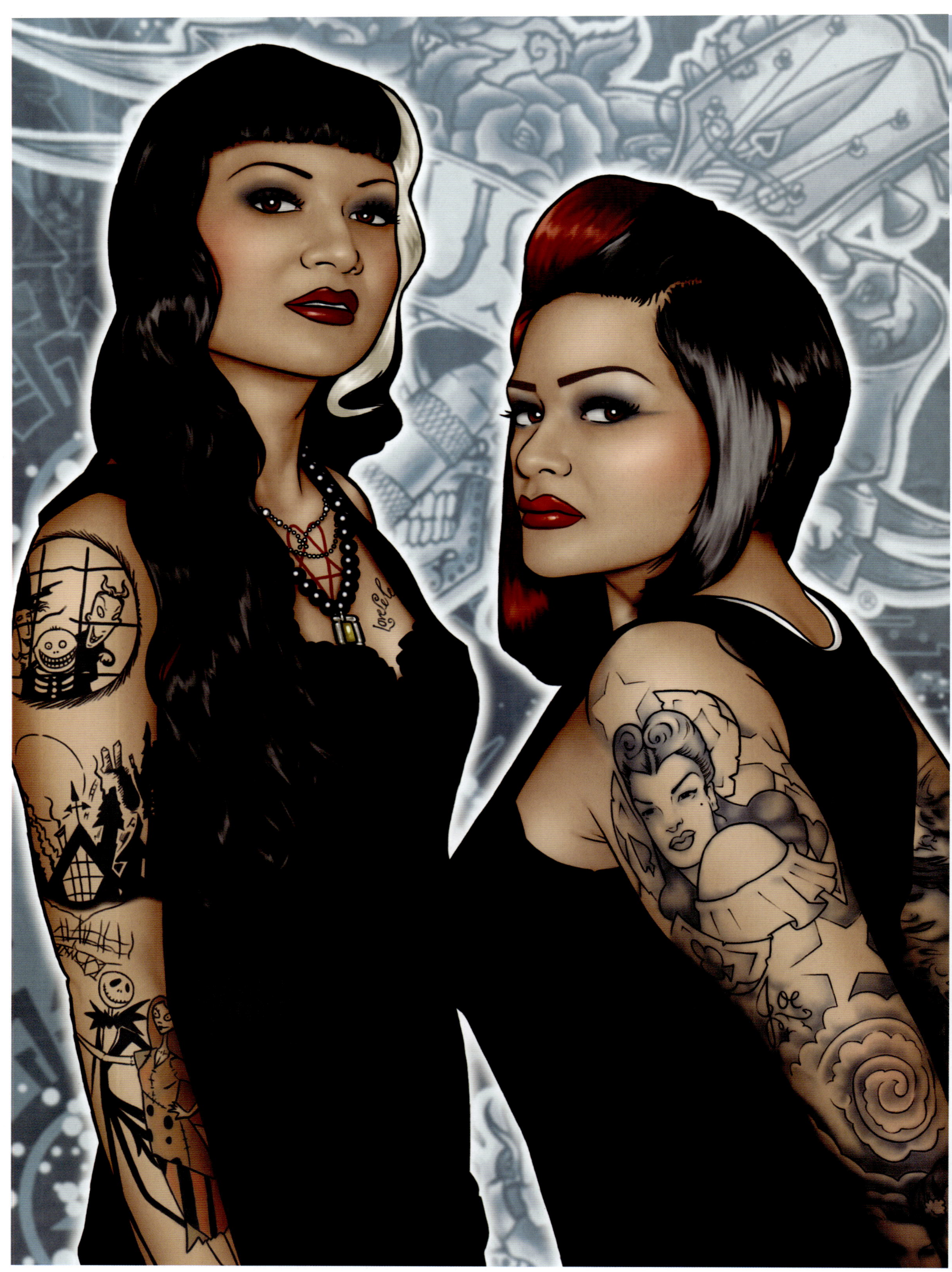
Lorelei
Joe

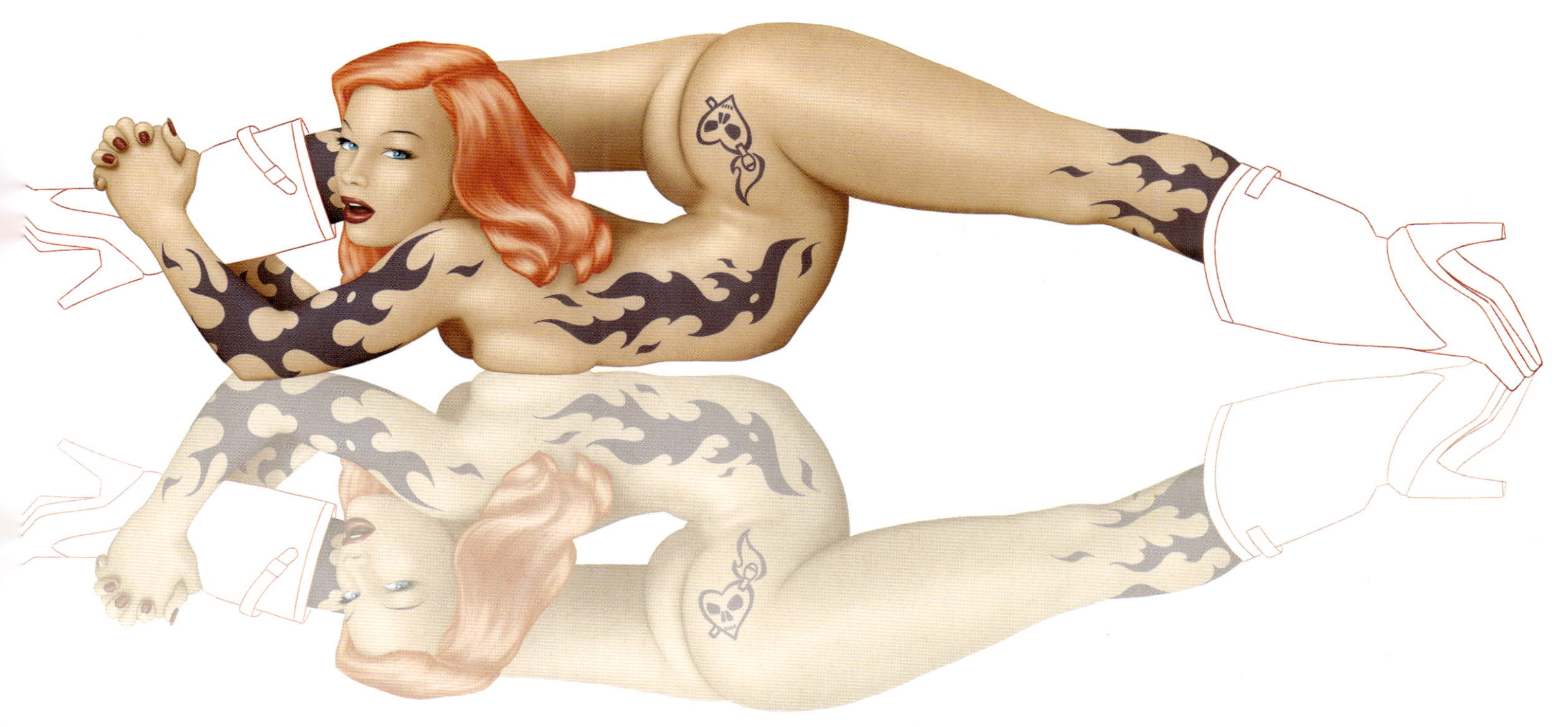

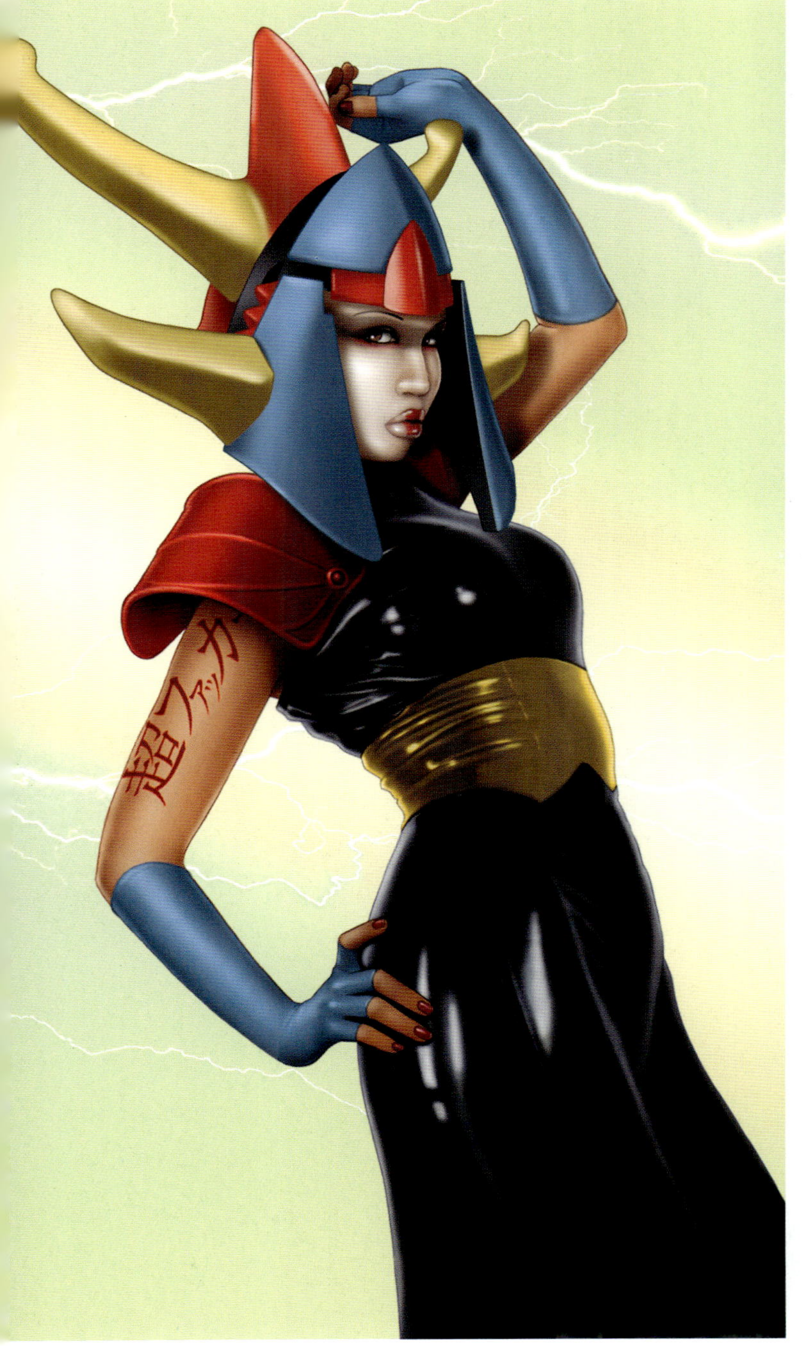
超ファッカ

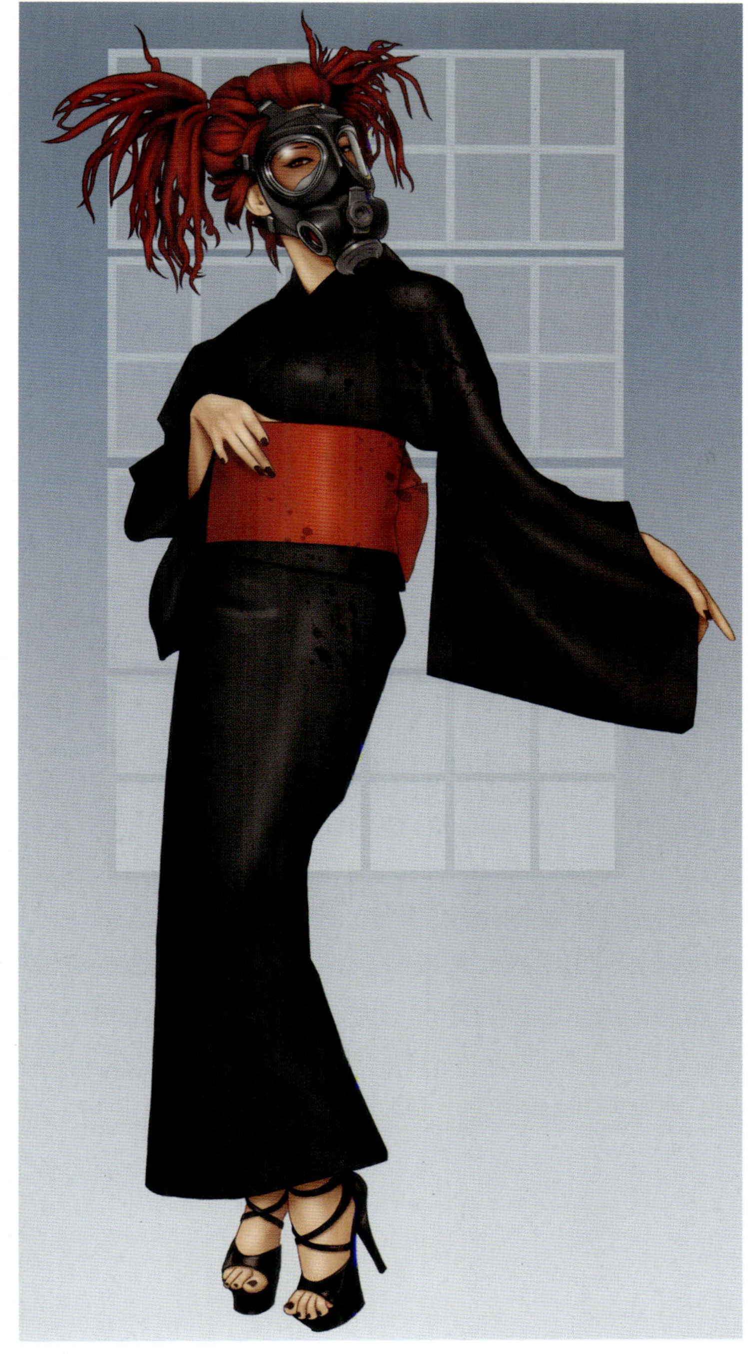

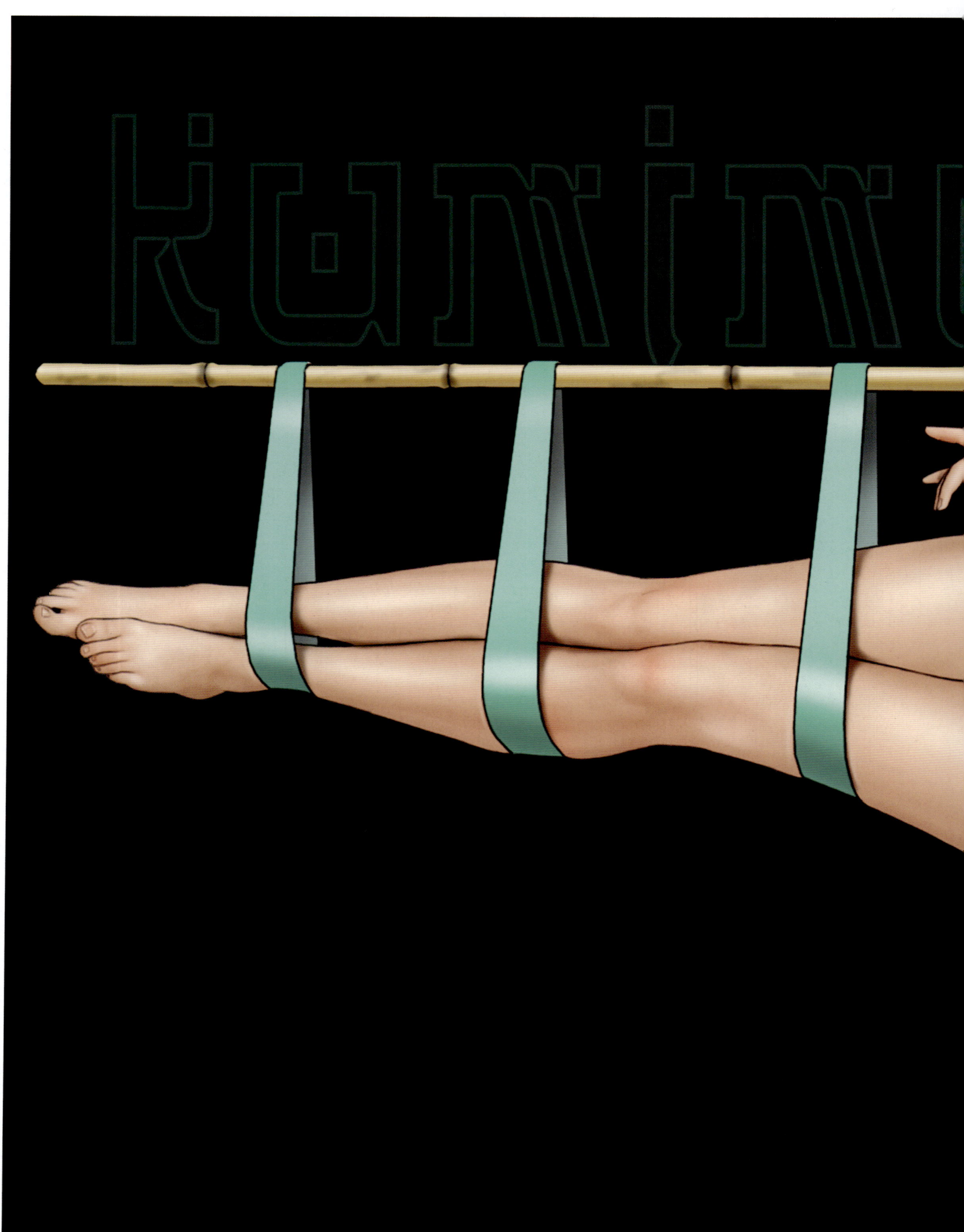

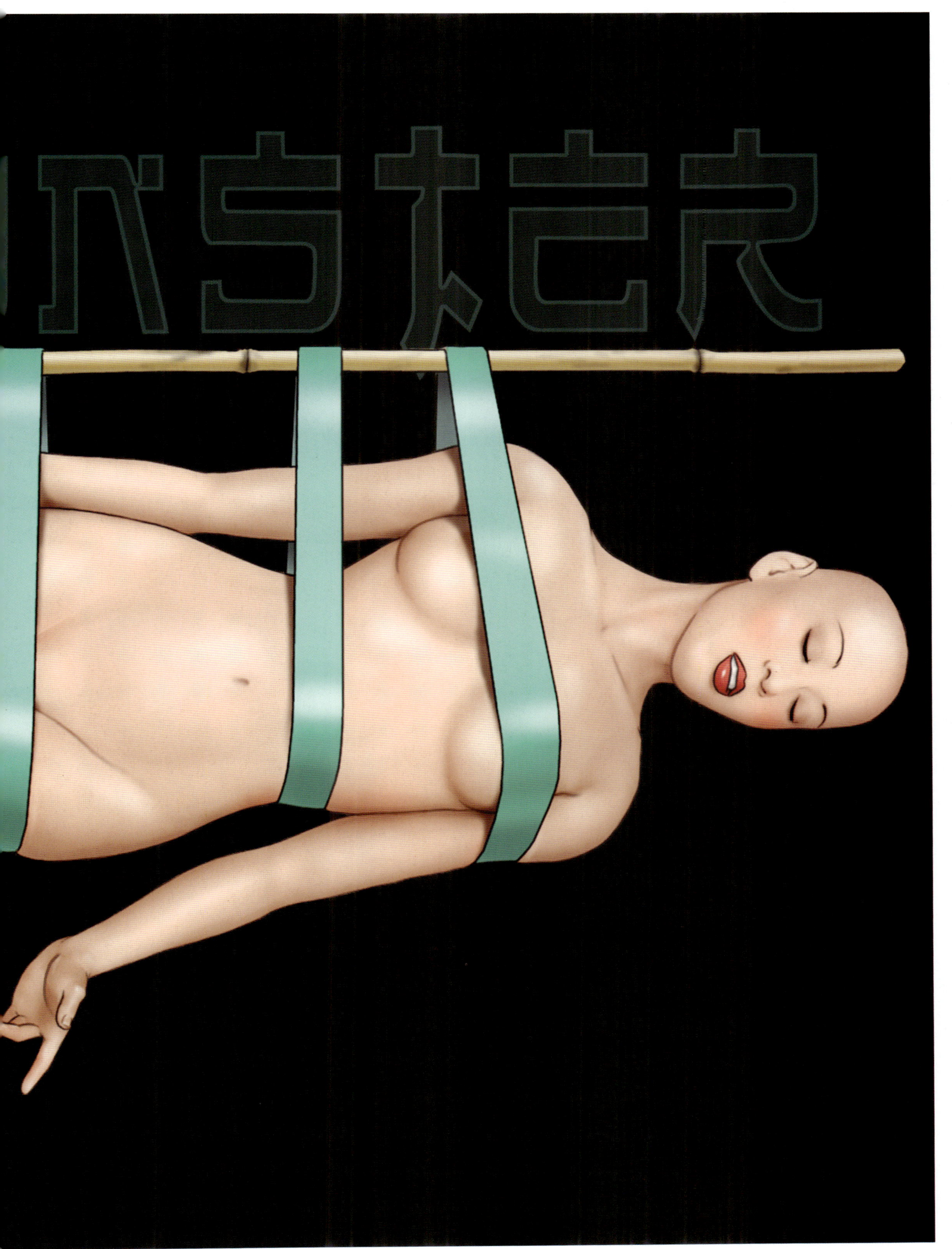
NSTER

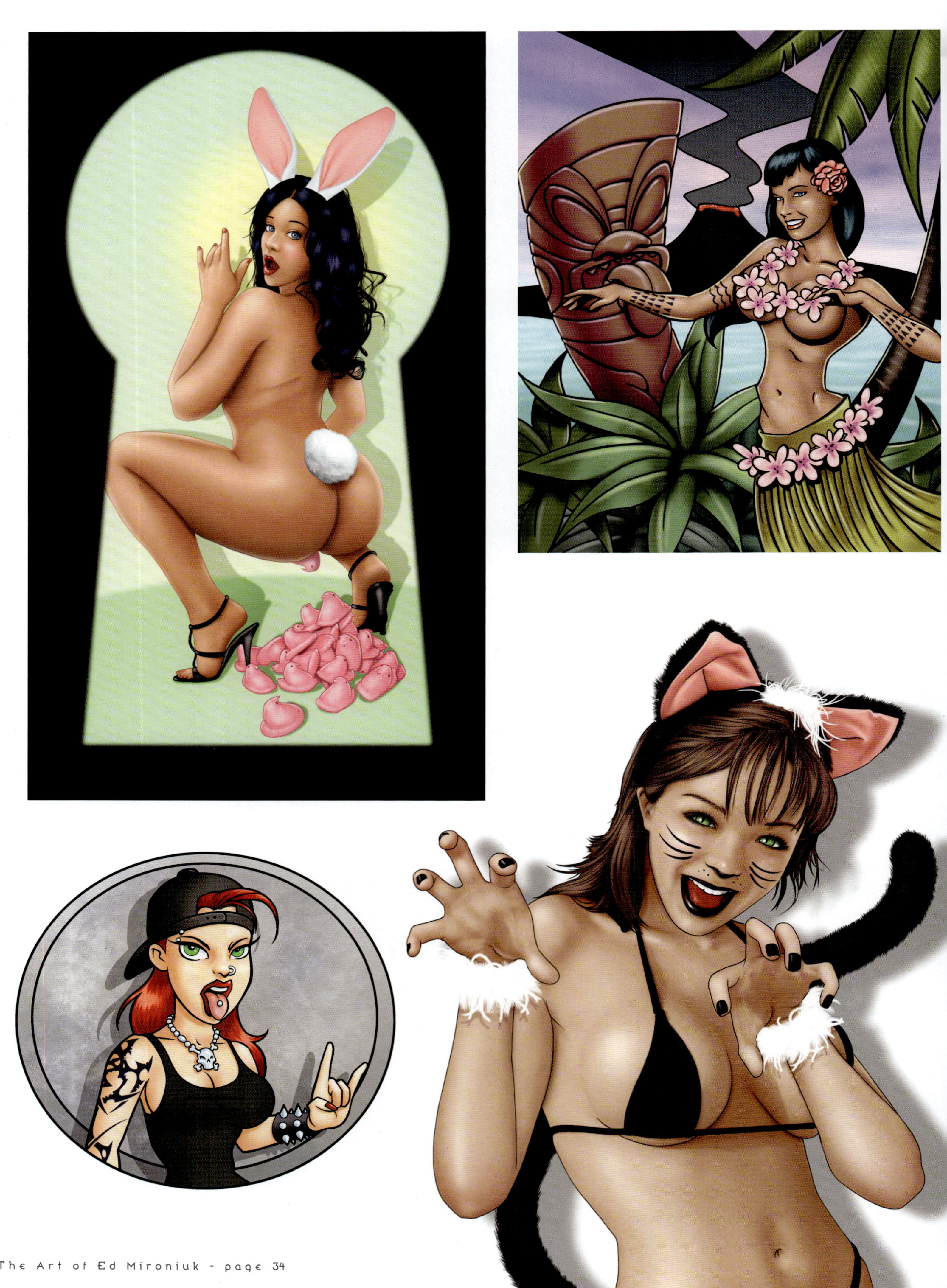

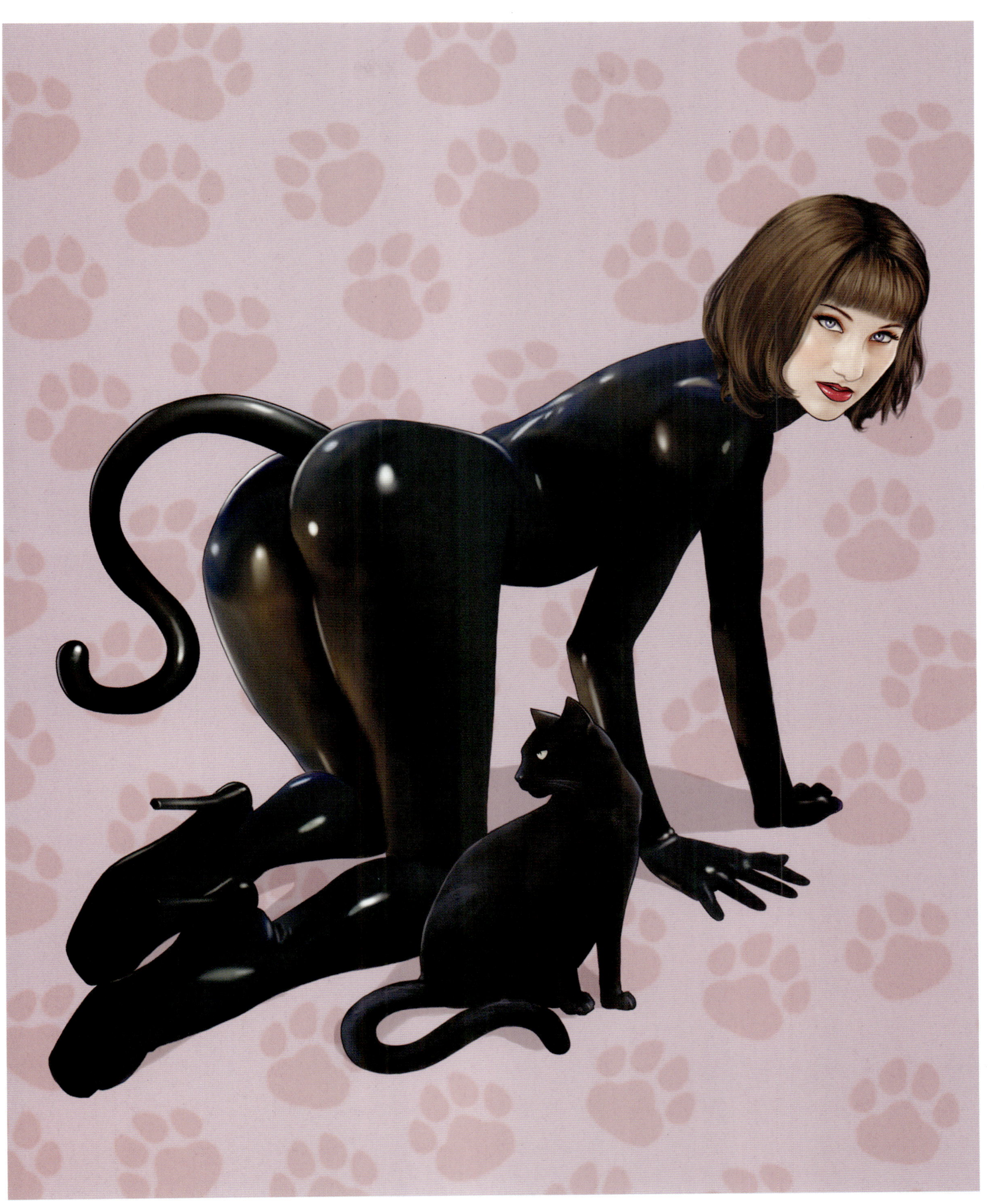

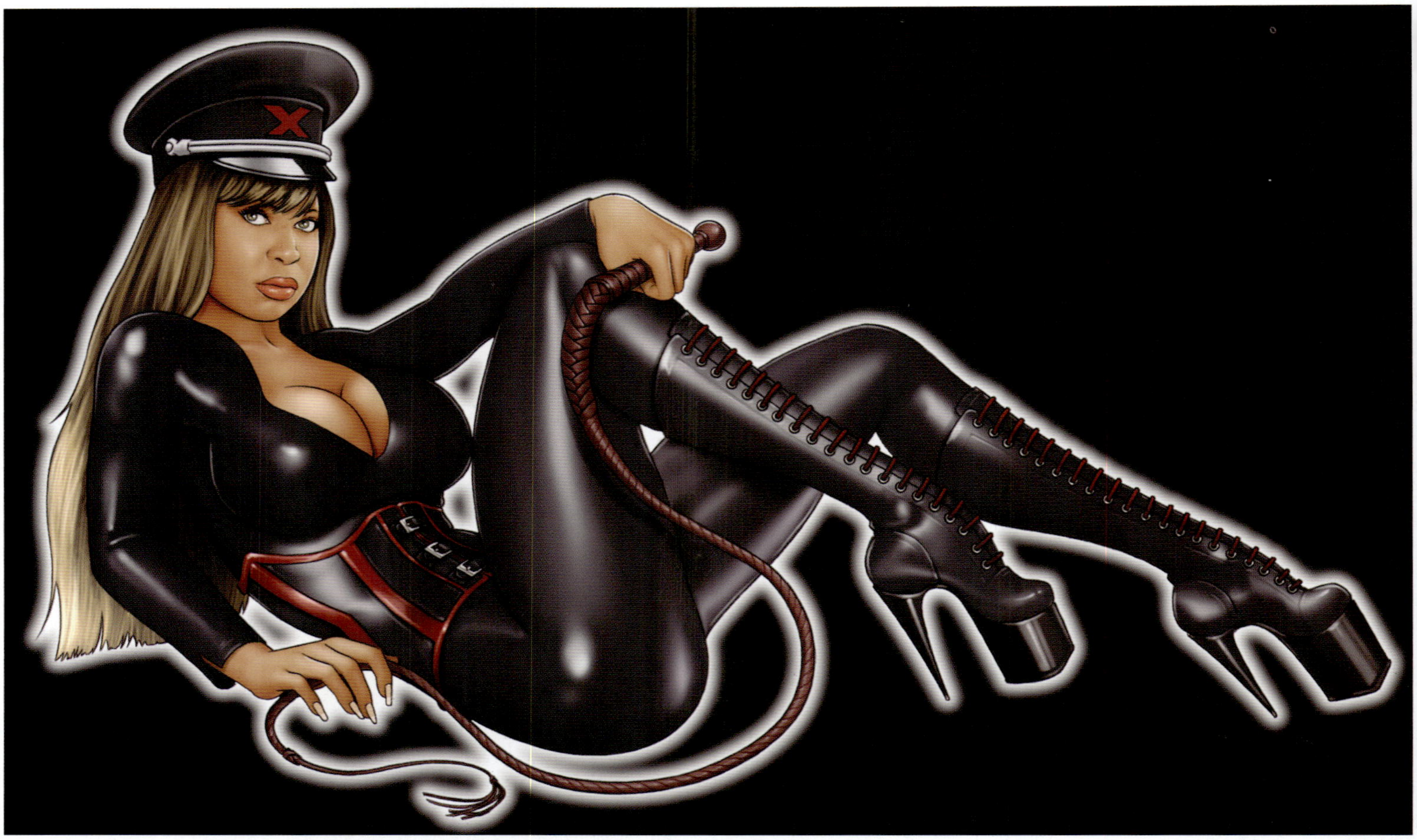

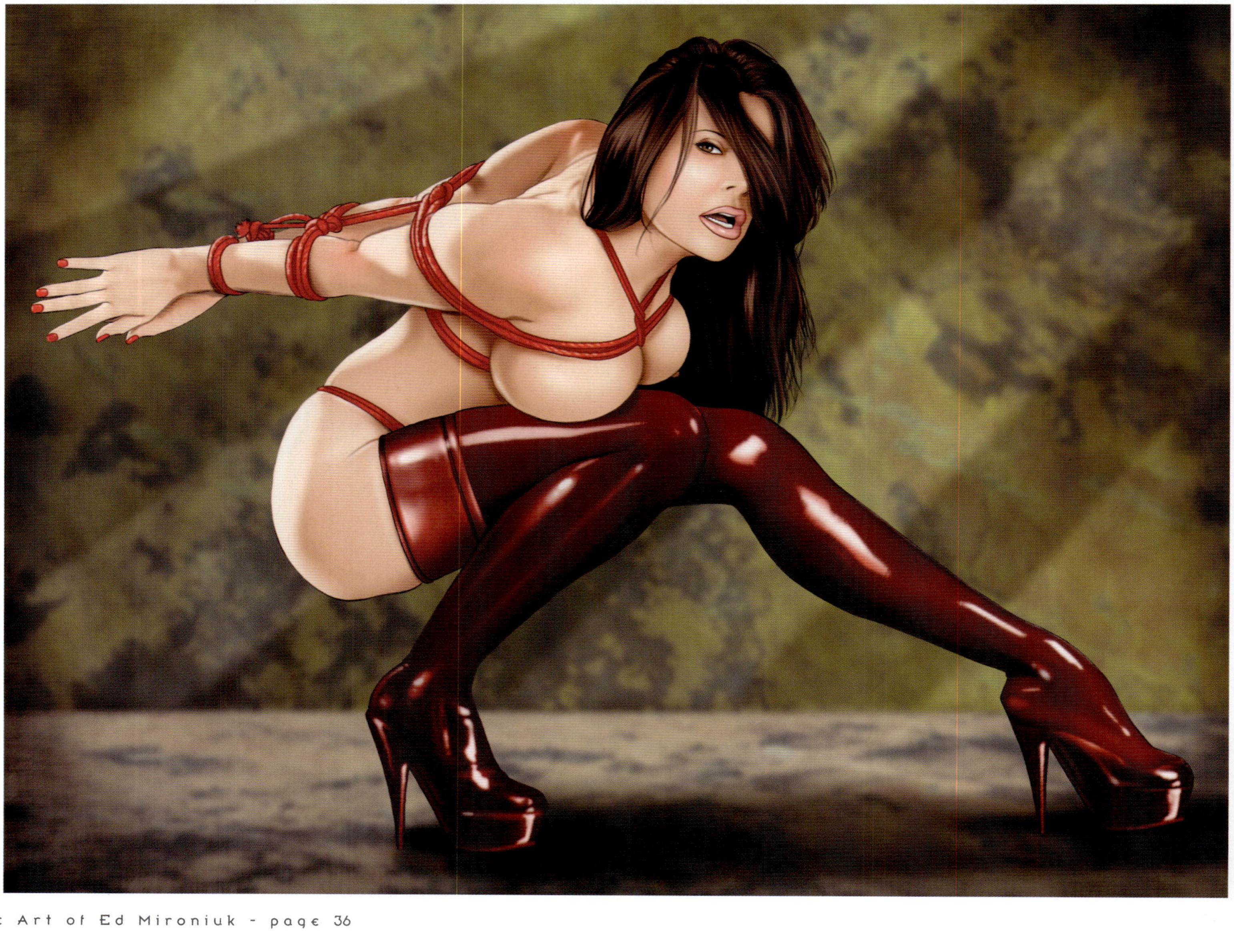

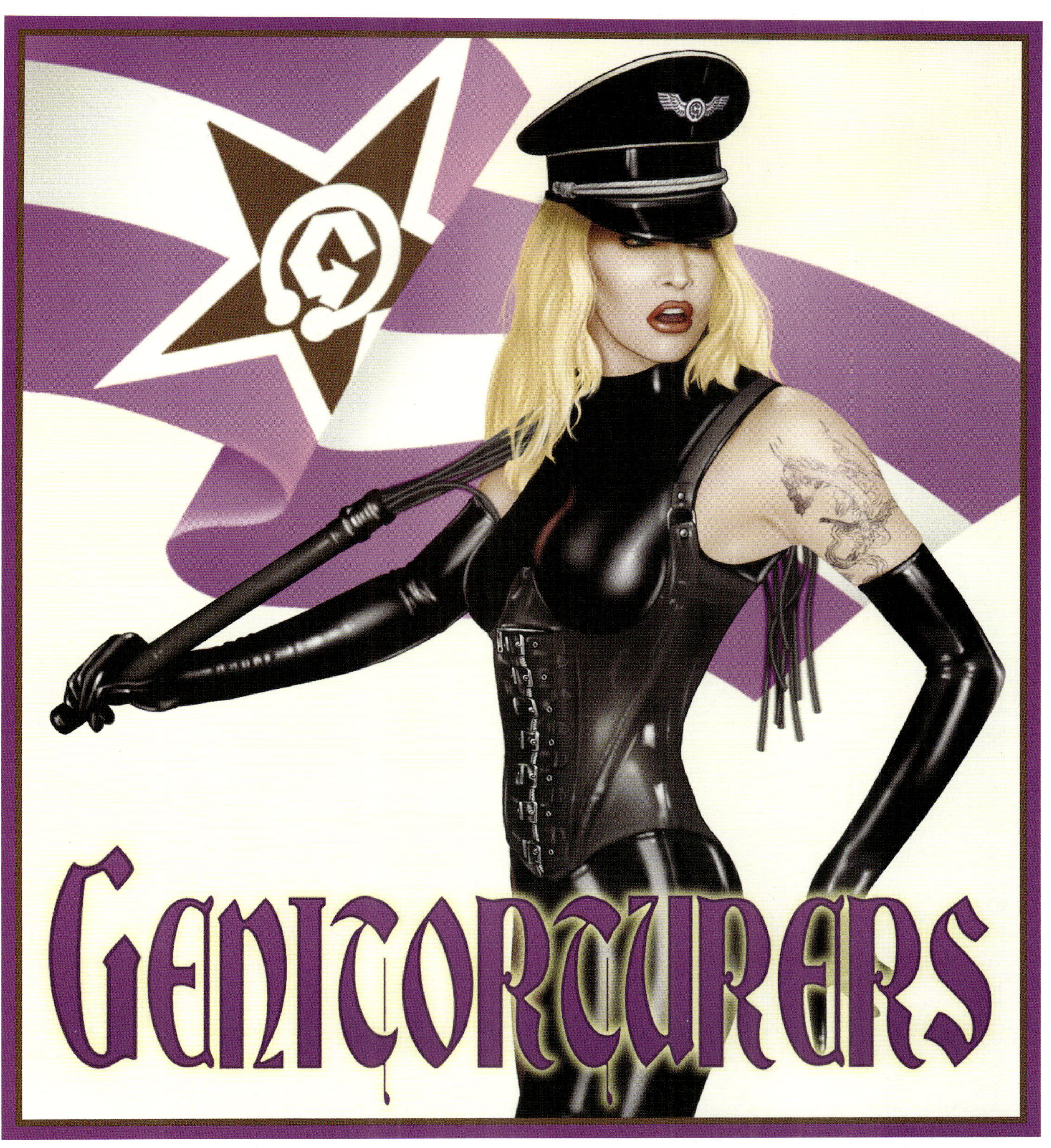
GENITORTURERS

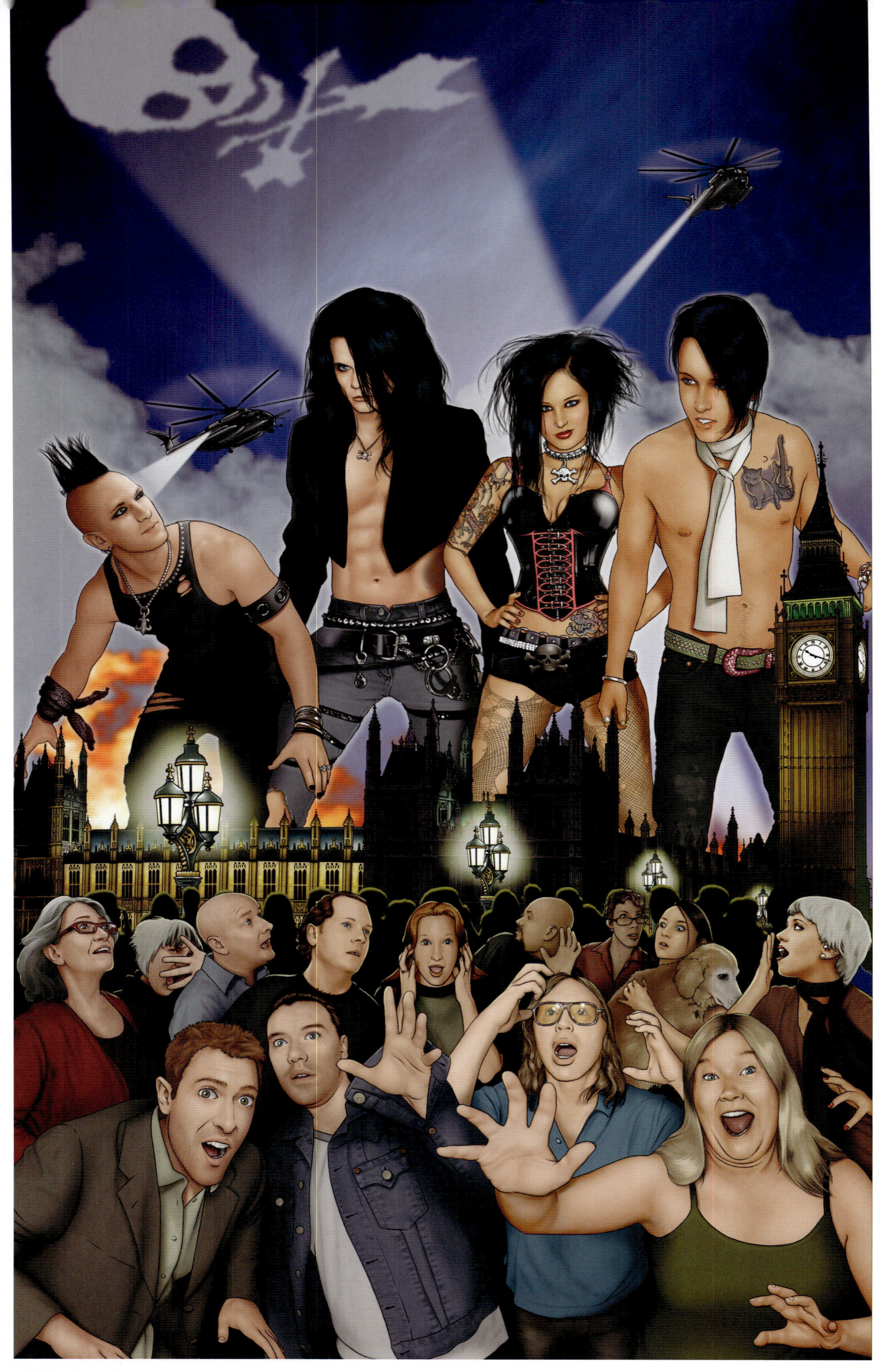

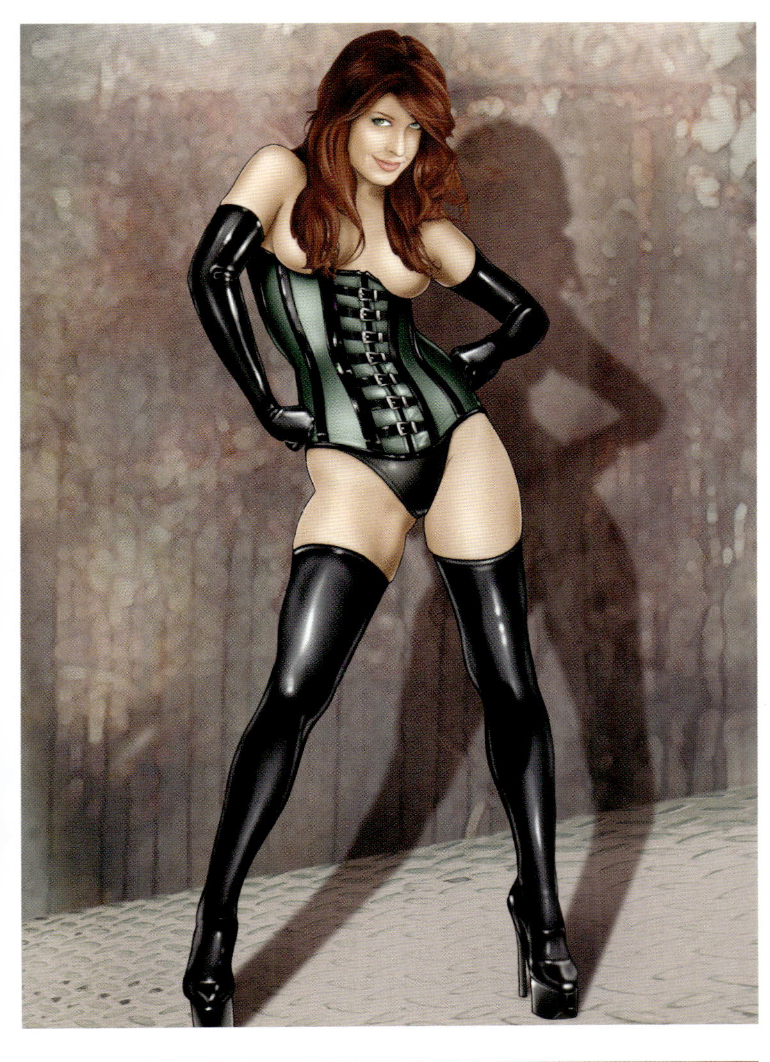

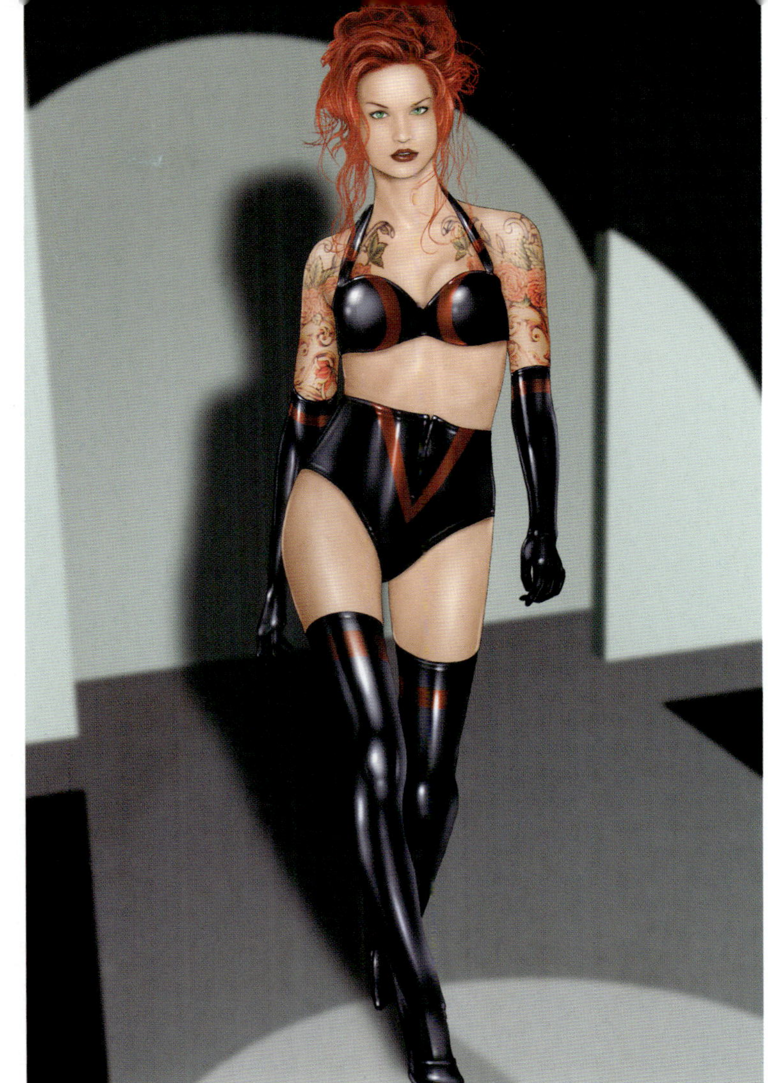

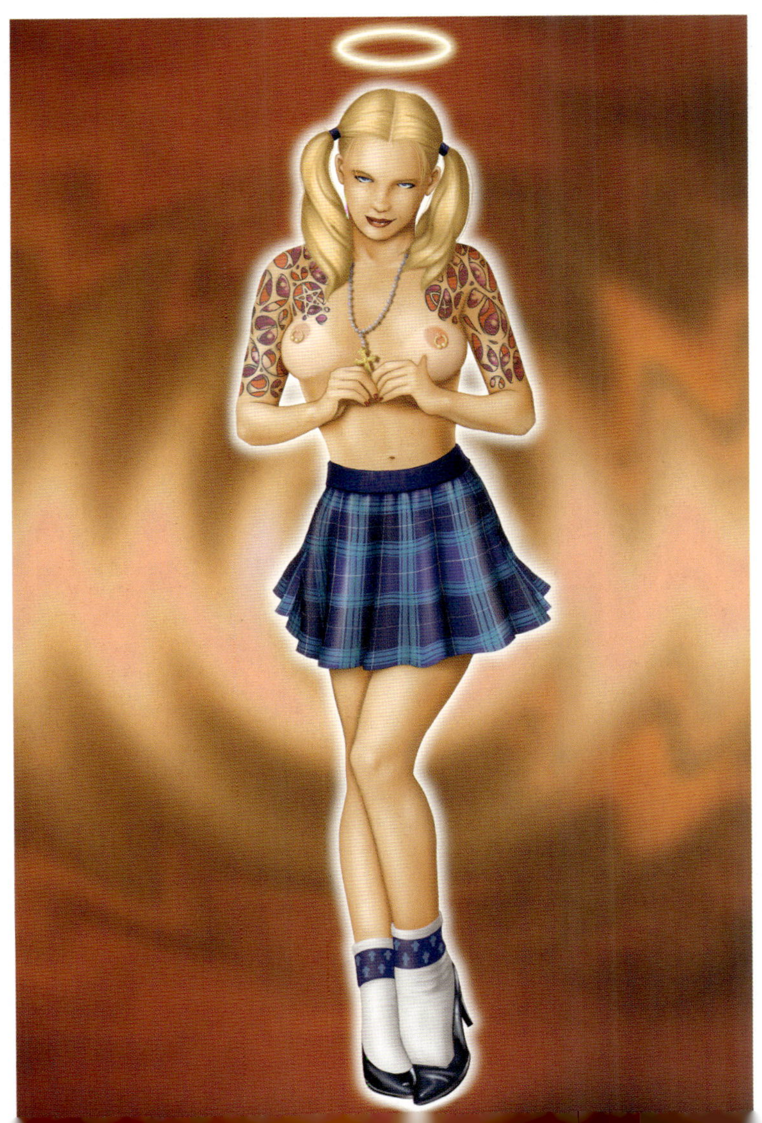

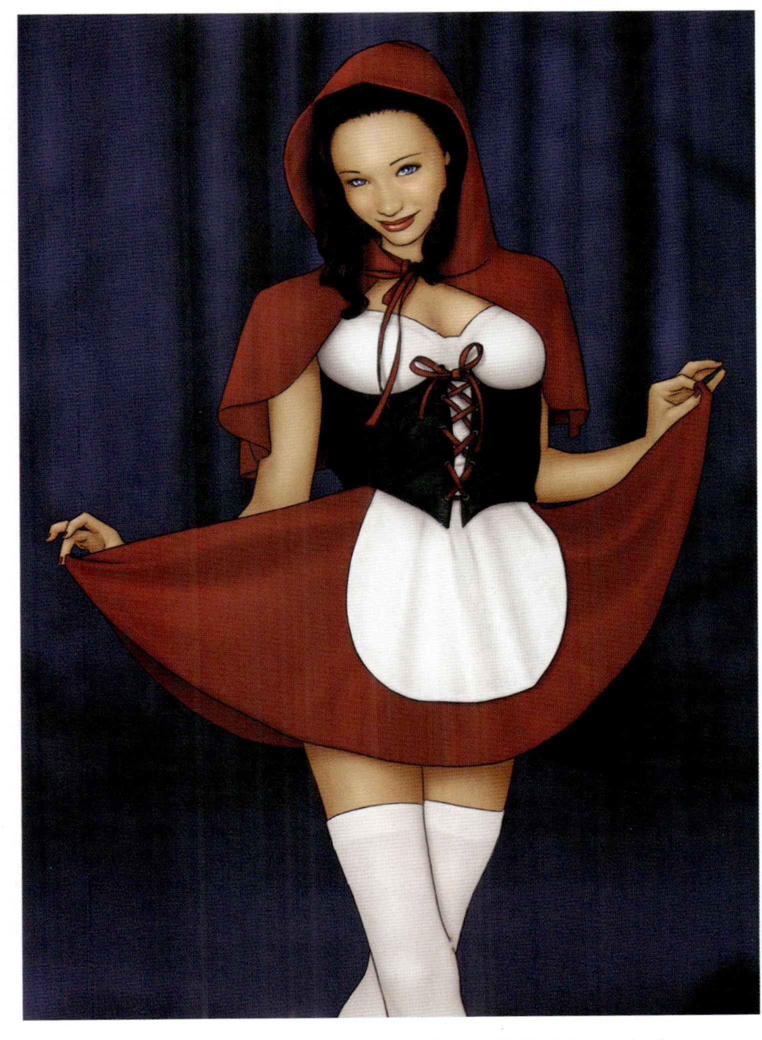

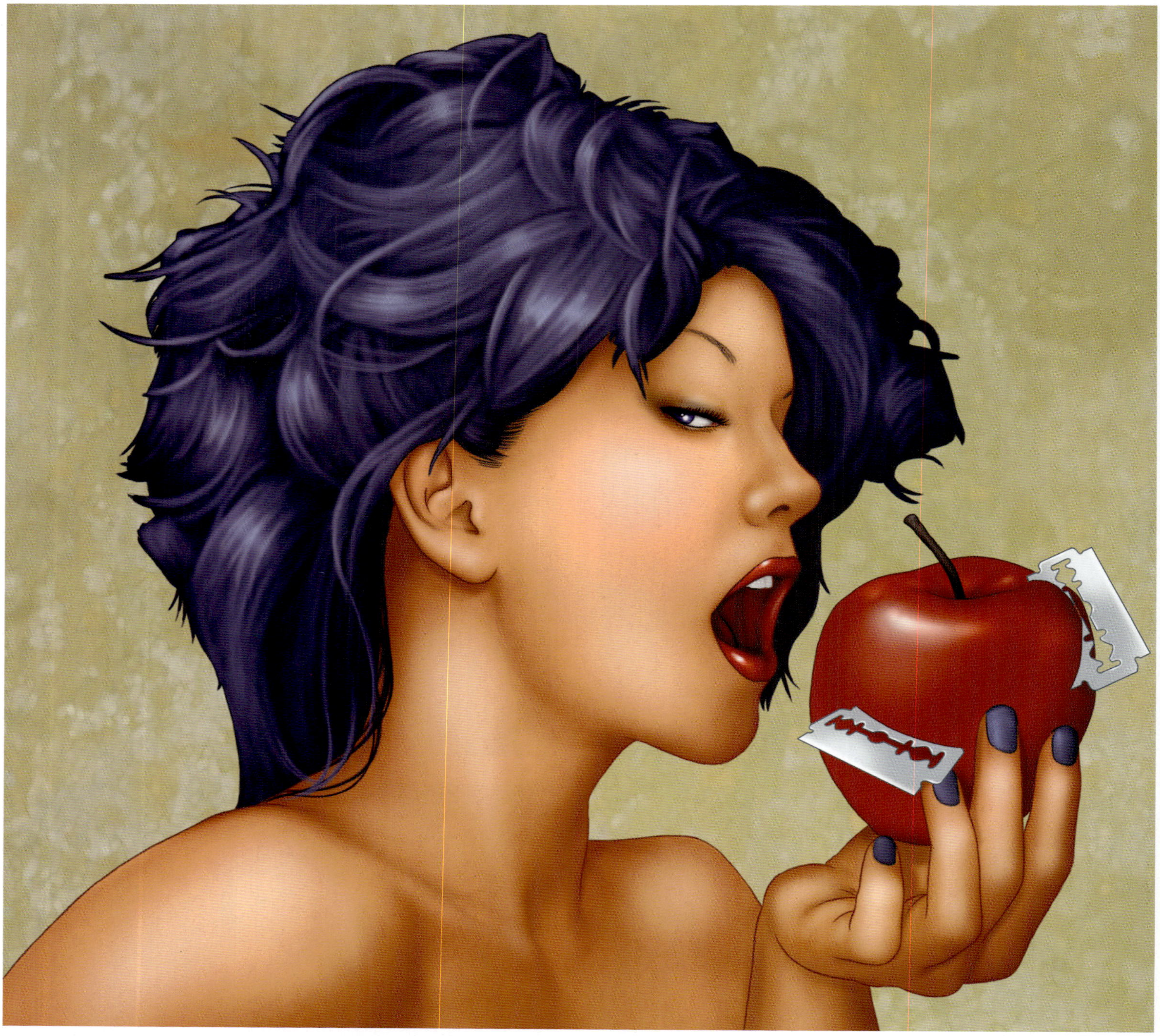

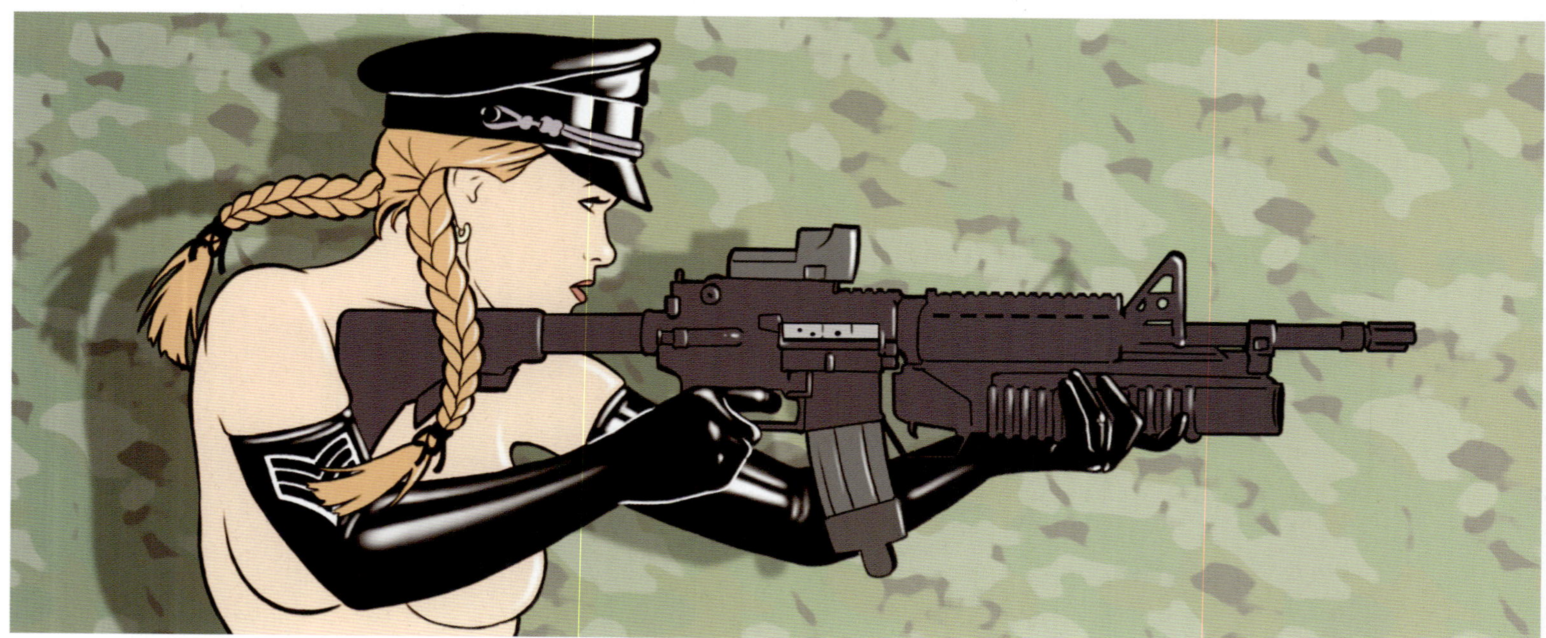

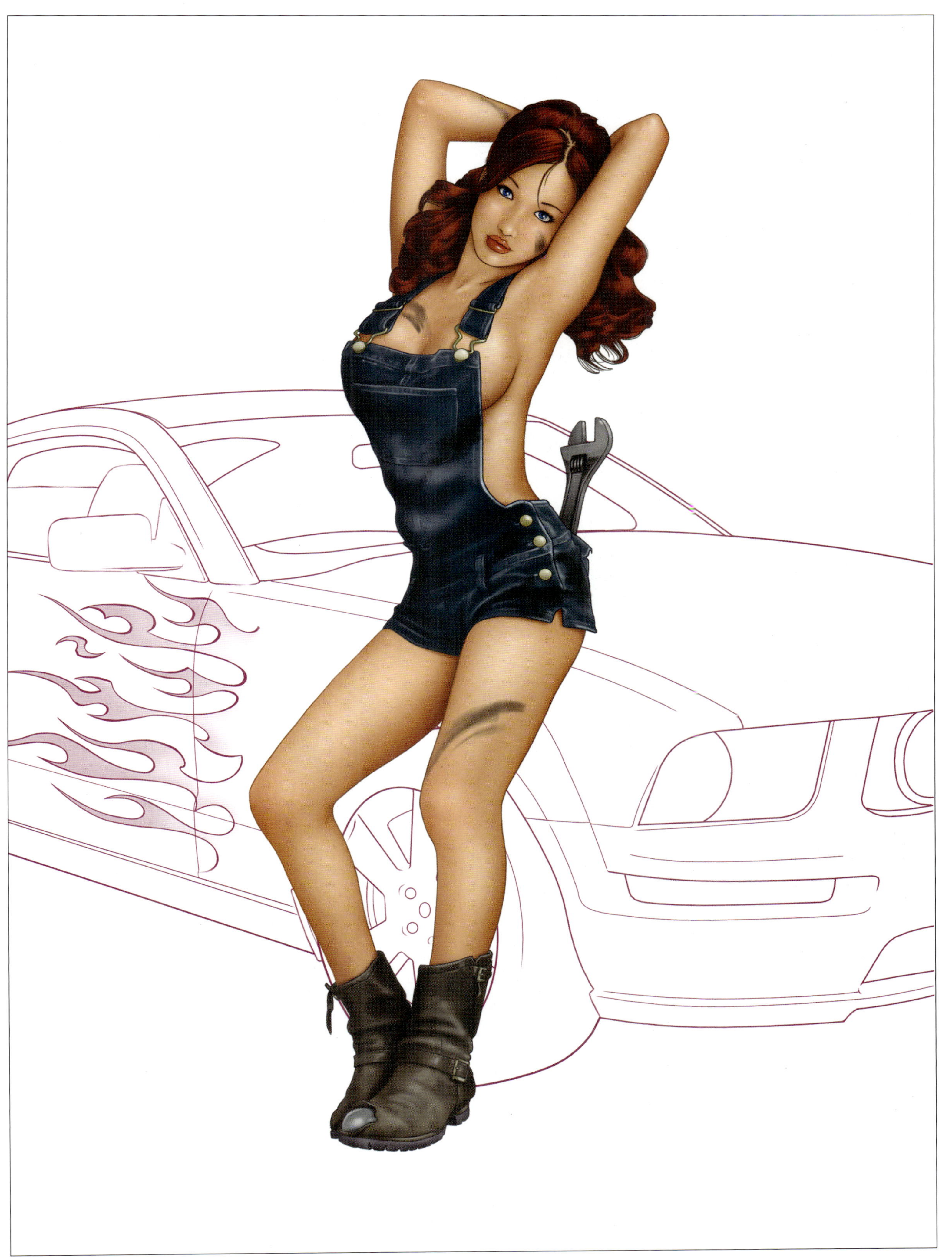

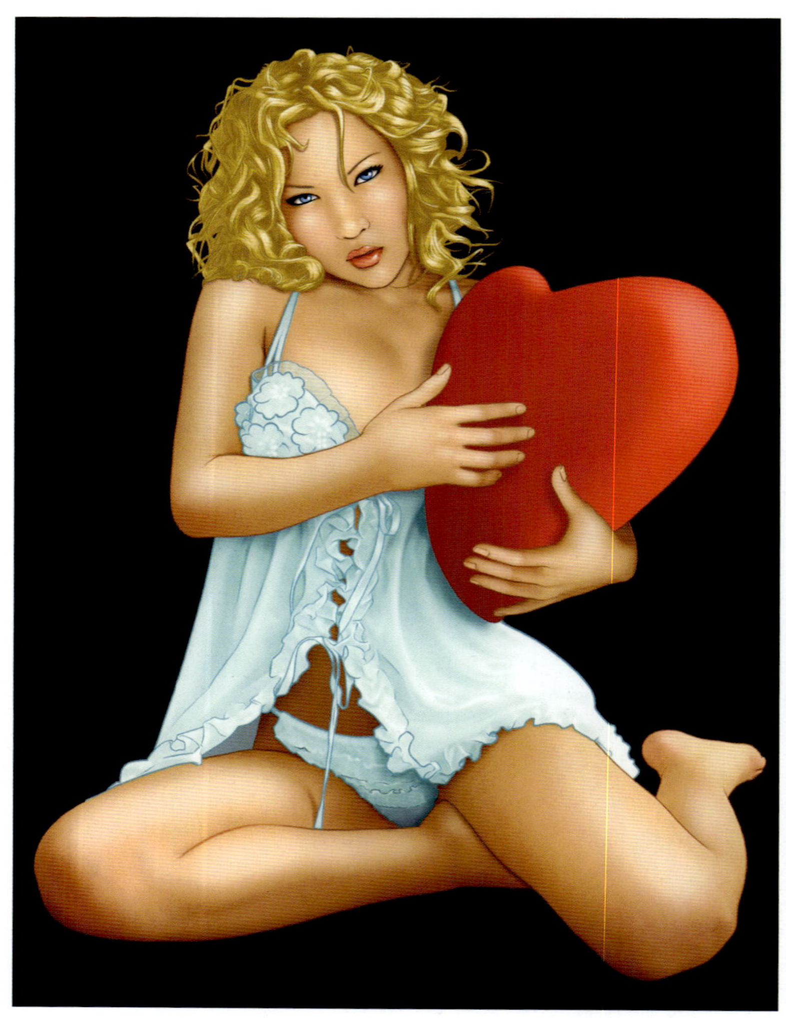
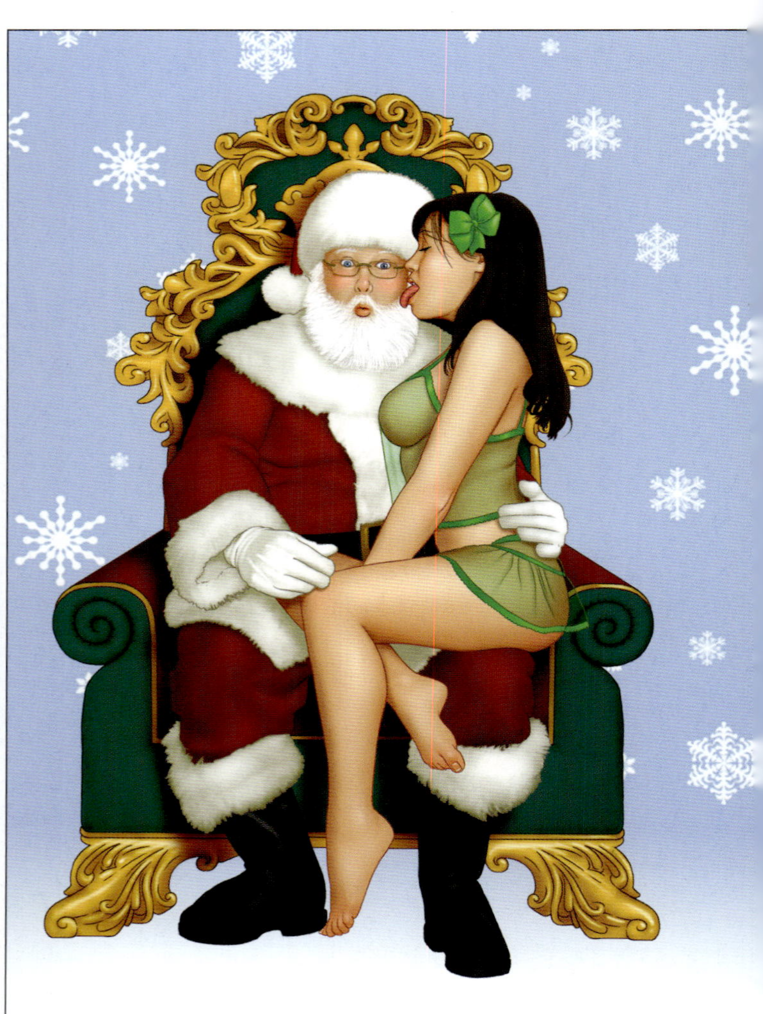
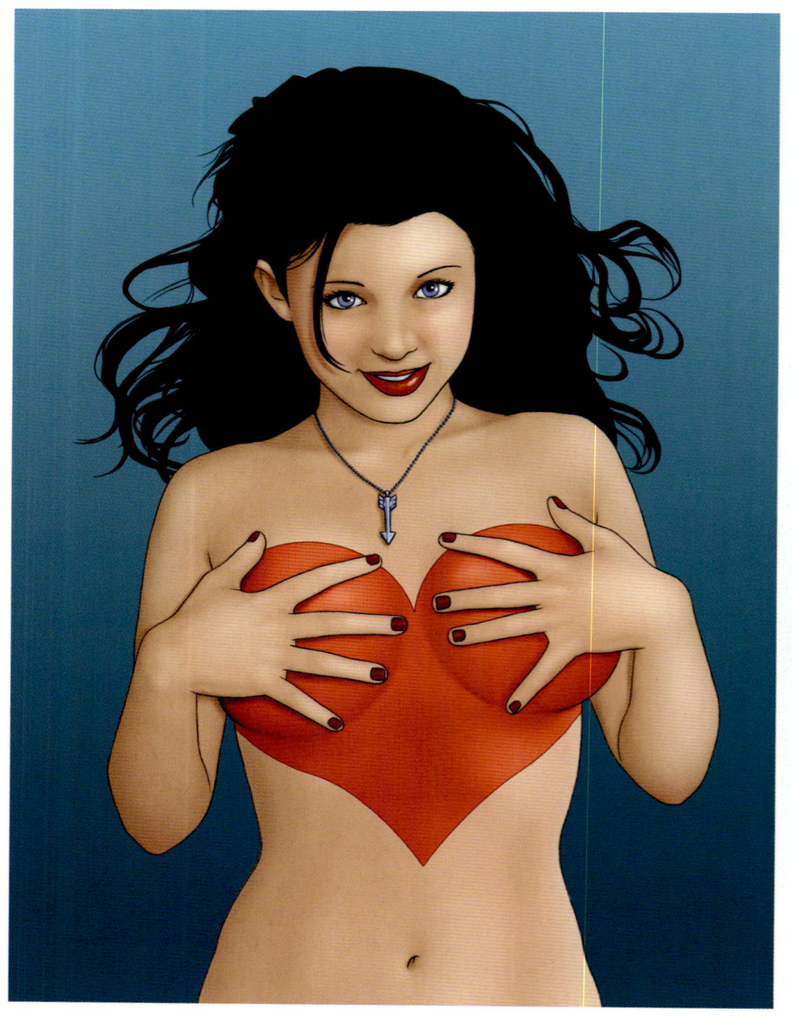
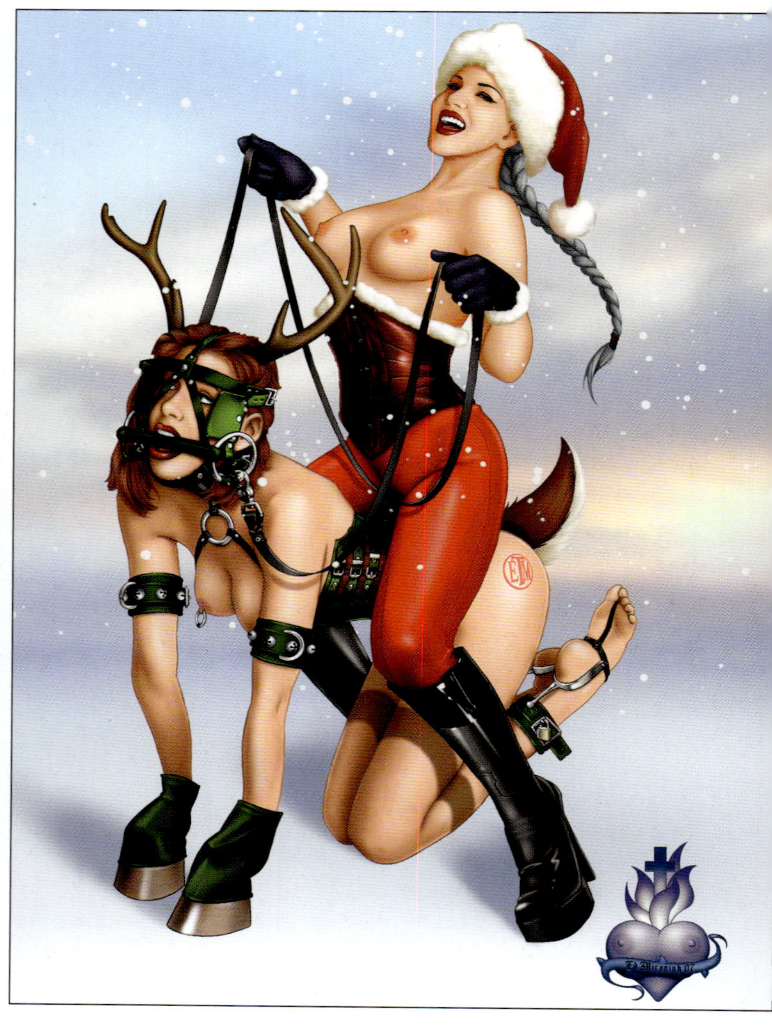

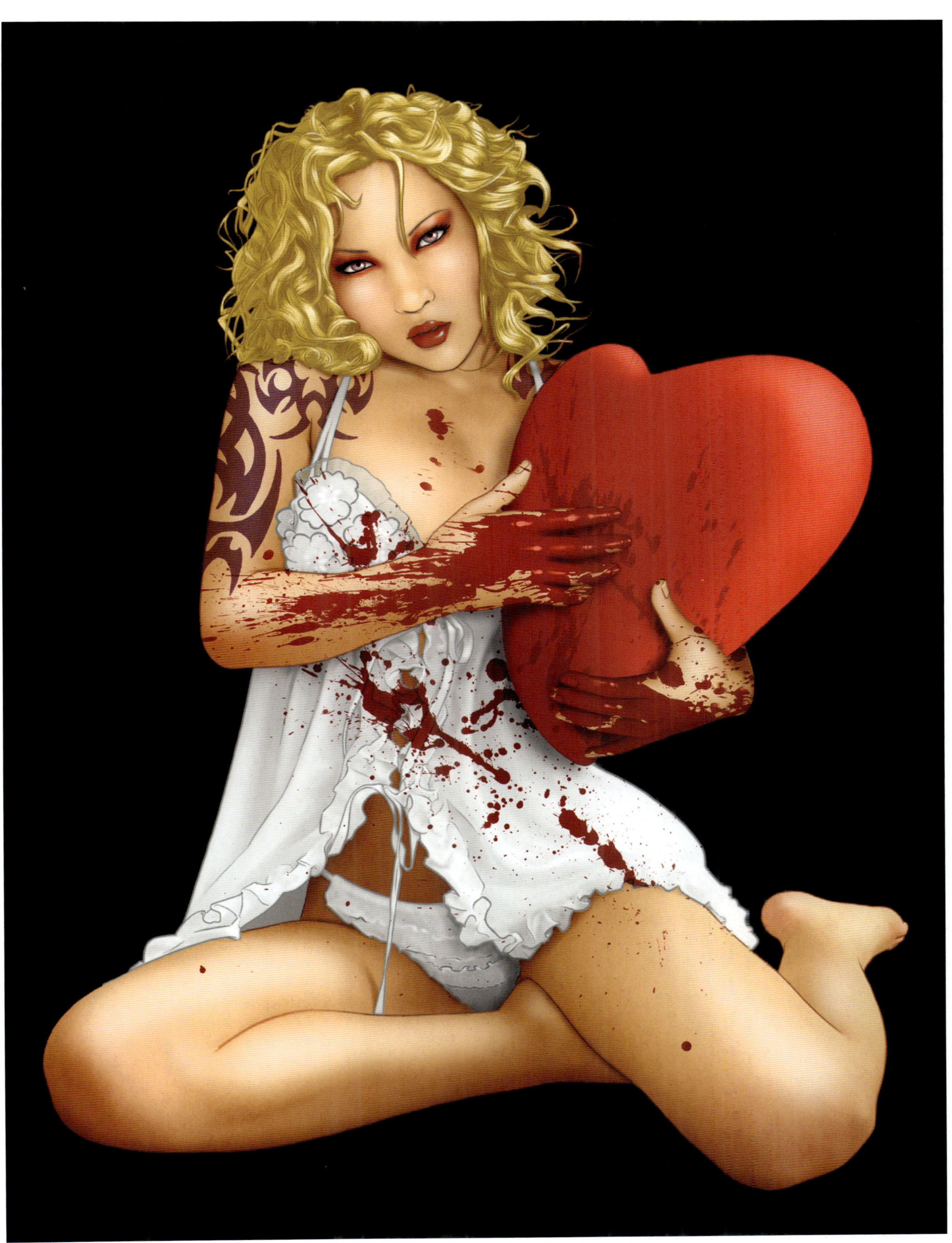

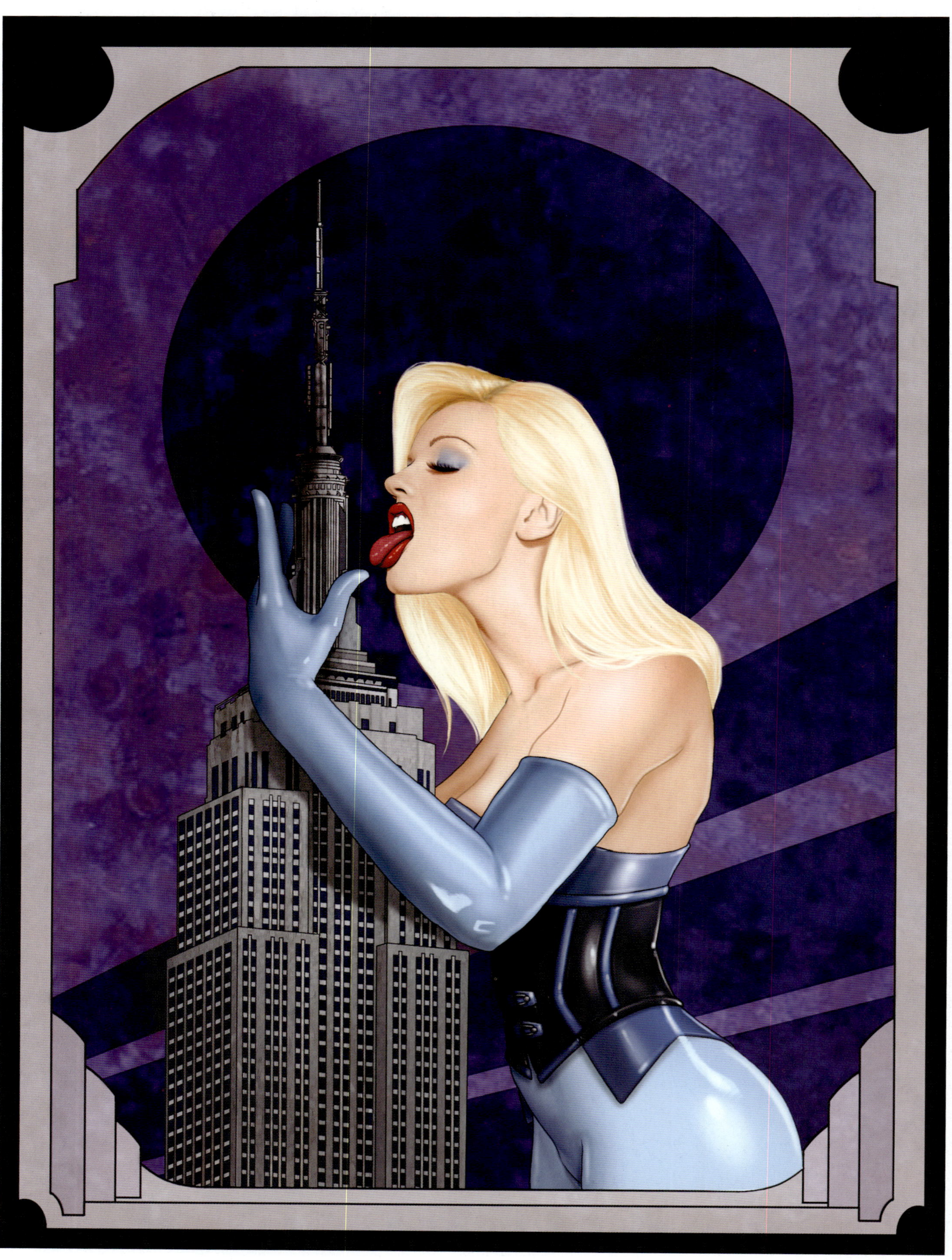

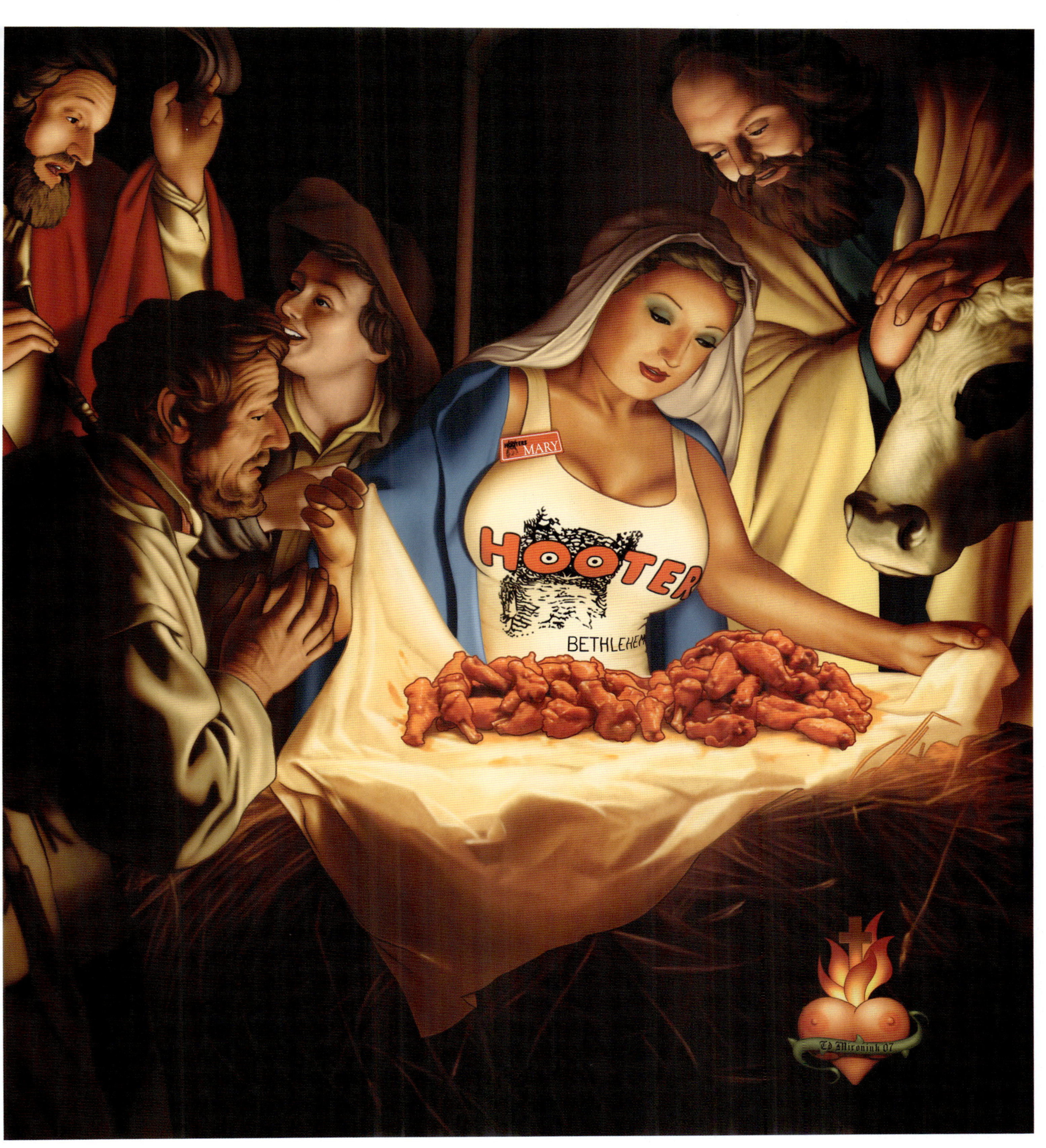
MARY
HOOTER
BETHLEHEM
Ed Mironiuk 07

Ed's Got You Covered - Evolution of an Attitude!

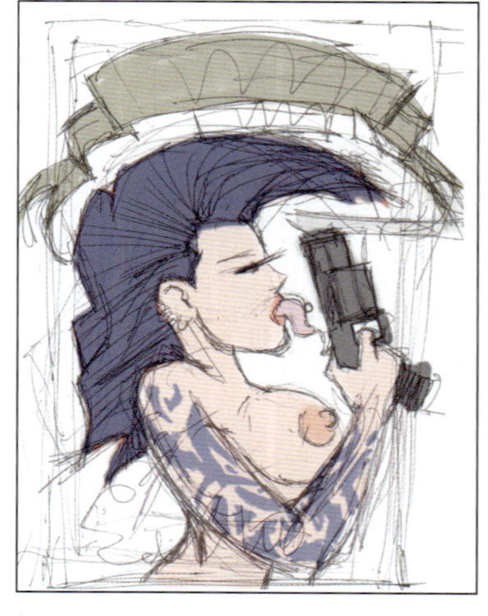
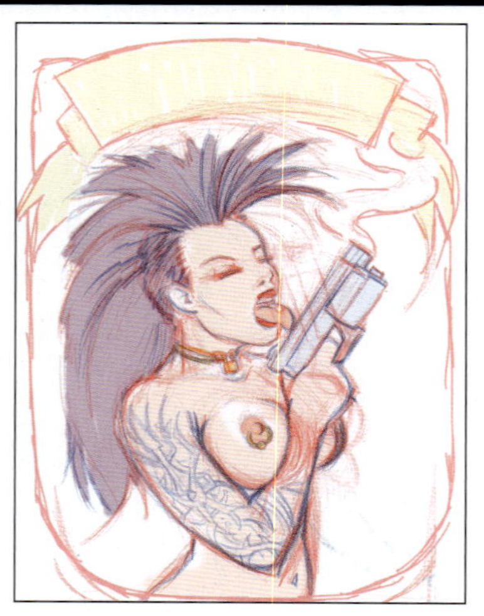
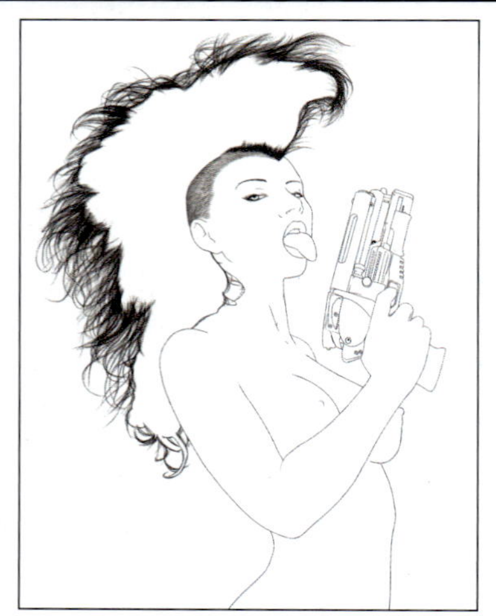
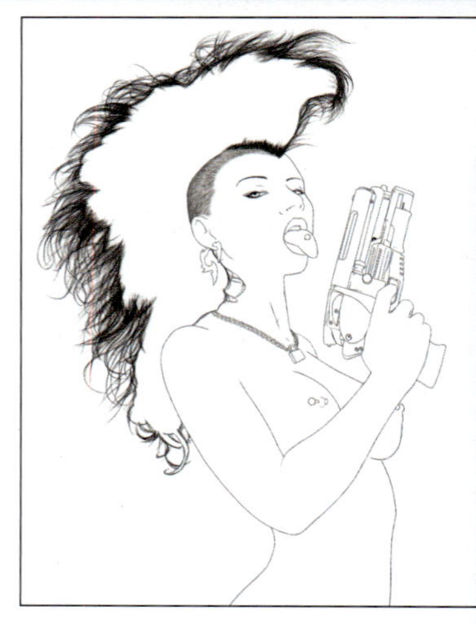
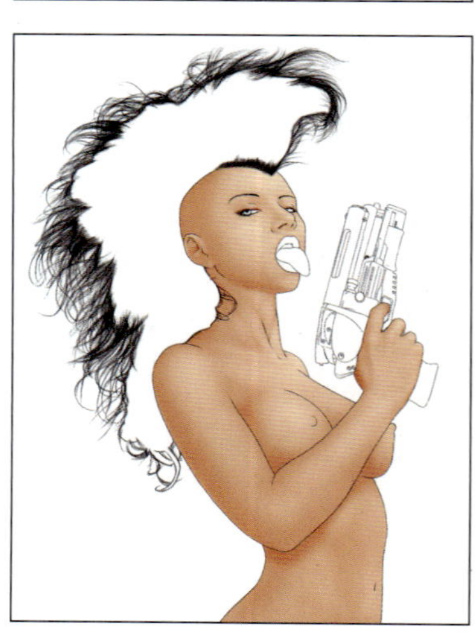
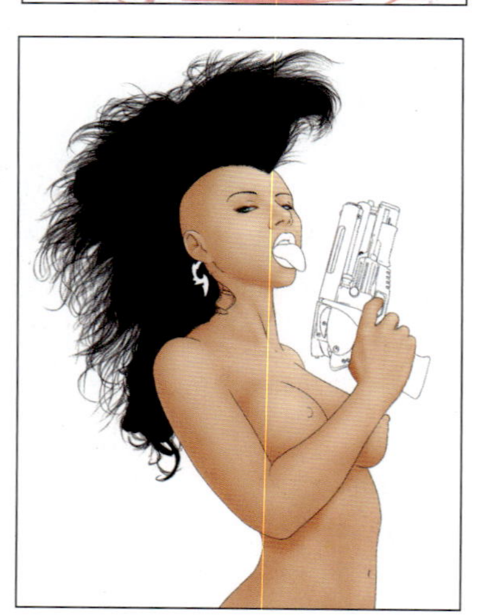
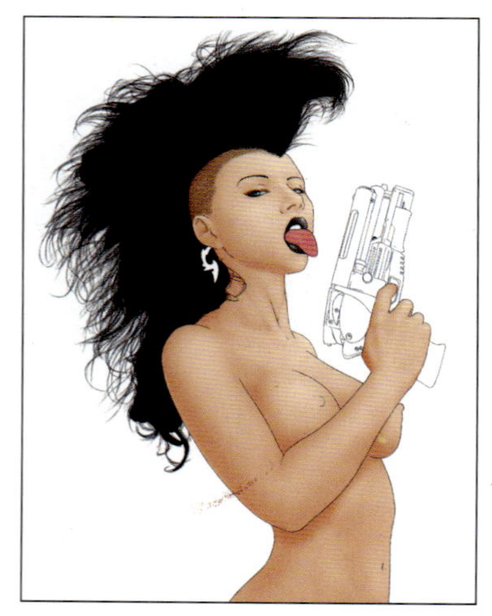
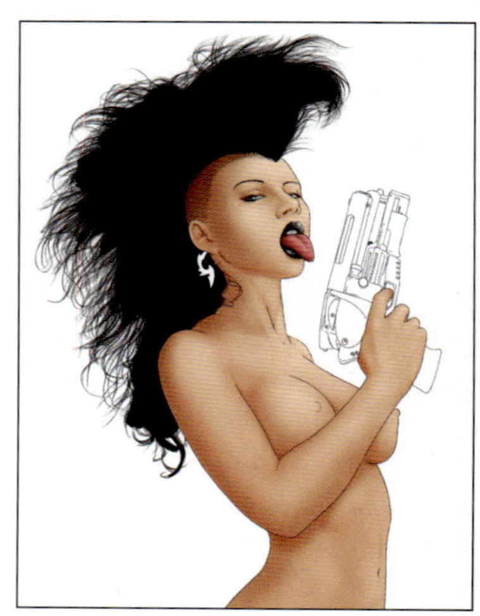
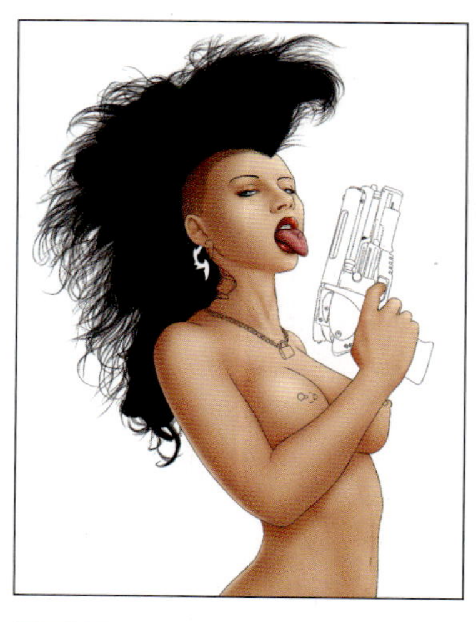
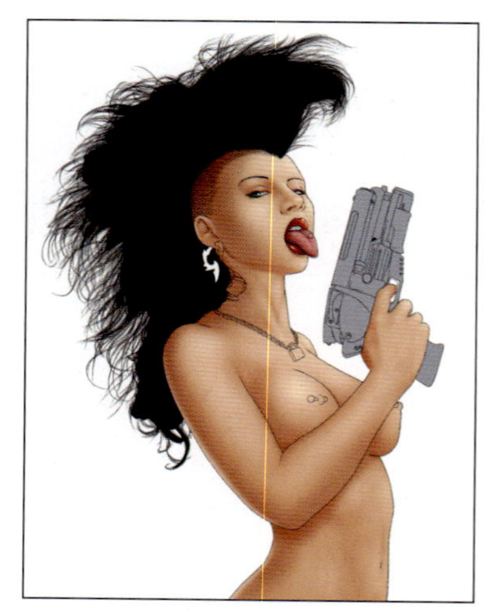
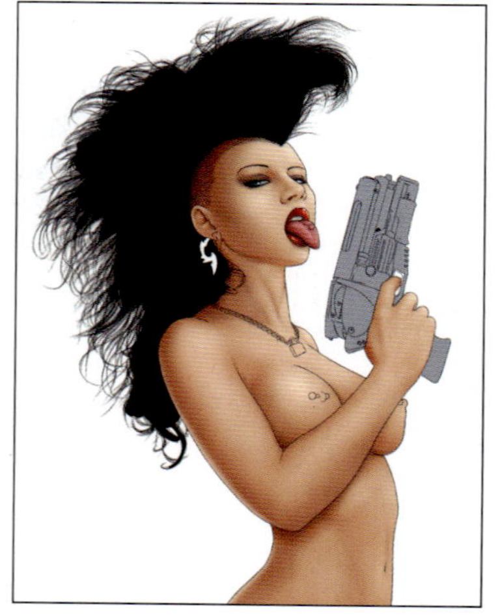
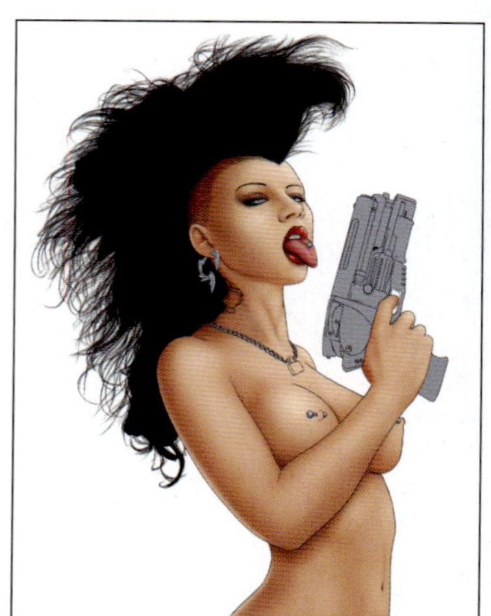
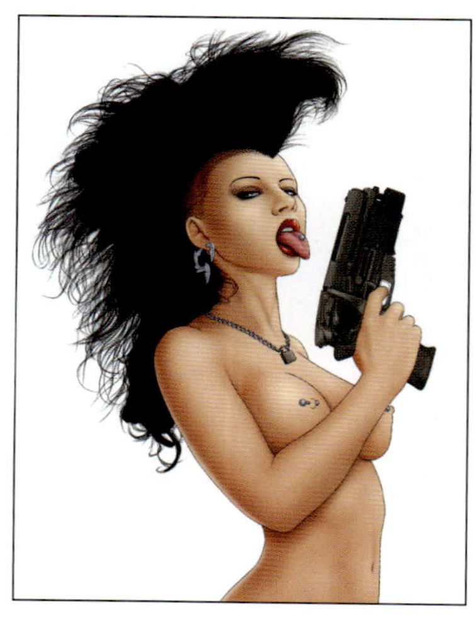
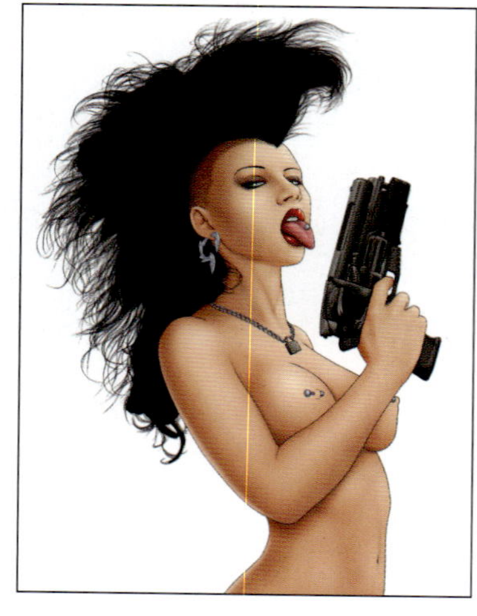
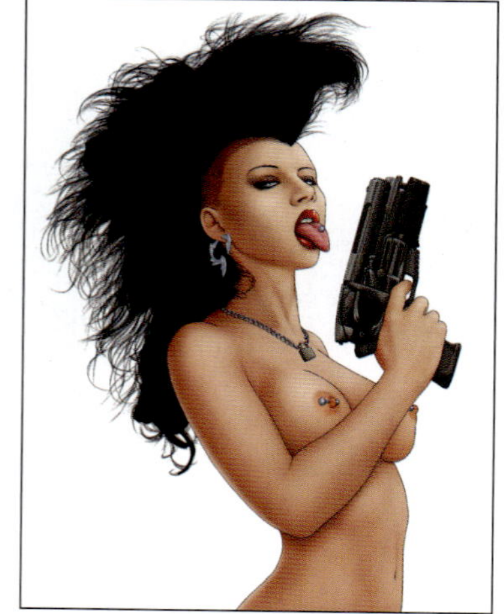
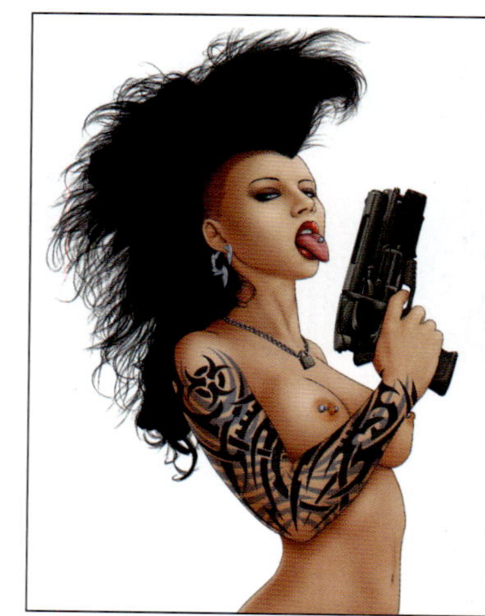

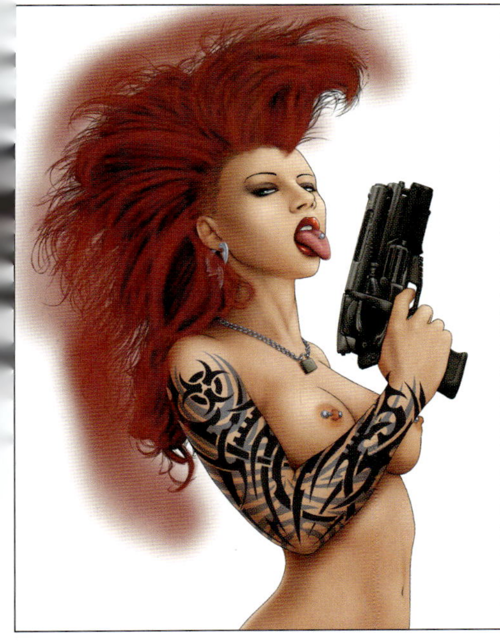
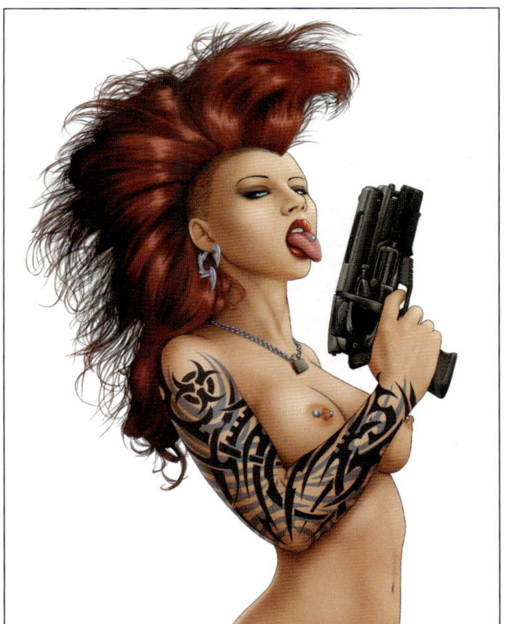
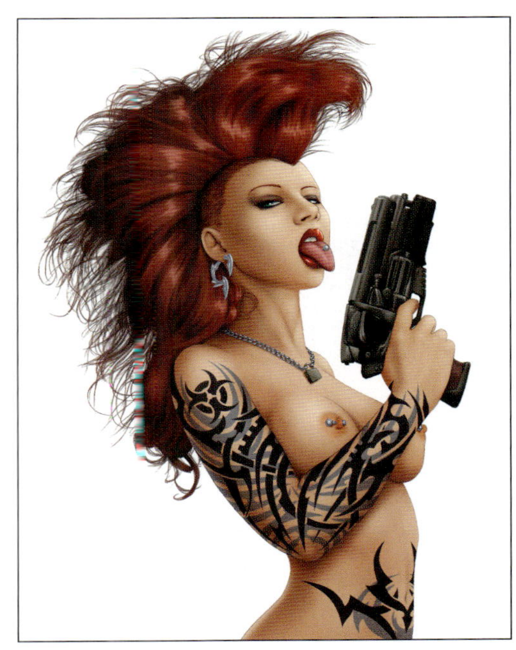
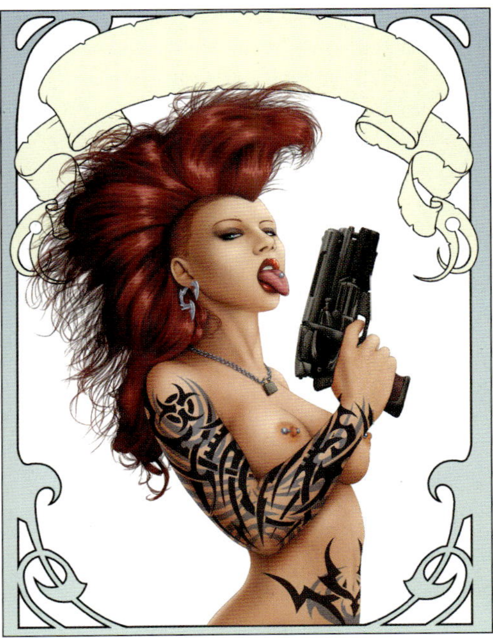
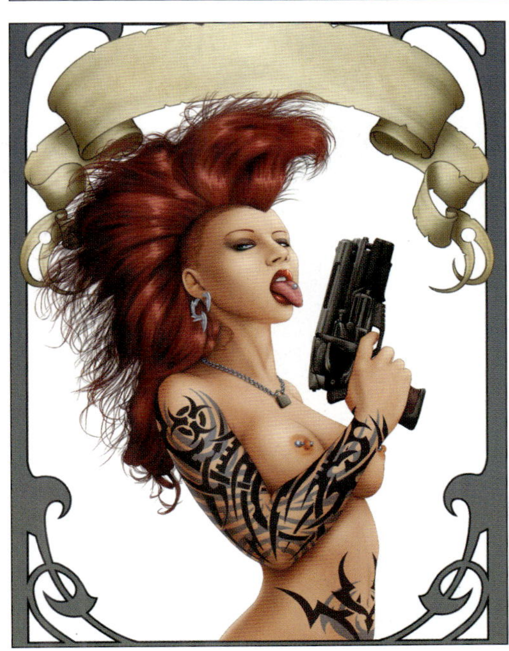
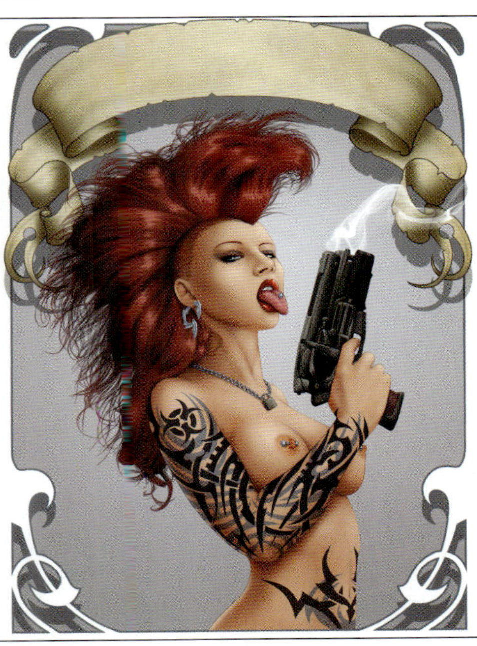

When I started this, I wanted the cover art to reflect my personality and interests - dangerous hot chicks with tattoos and piercings, the kind of gal who would protect you after the apocalypse. After weeks of teeth gnashing and crying she came to me like the image of Jesus in a potato chip. I immediately pulled myself out the fetal position from under the bed and after a few initial sketches, I had my hot little bad-ass ready to lay out. I armed her with a heavy-duty handgun, and worked an intricate two-color tribal tattoo. I sketched her out in pencil and finished her up in Photoshop. Lot's of layers and mattes for the shading and highlights and lots of color tweaking. Lather rinse repeat. I hope you enjoy looking at her as much as I did drawrin' her.

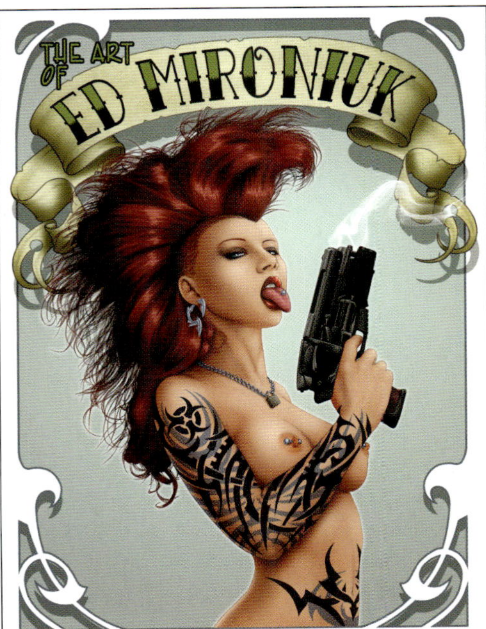

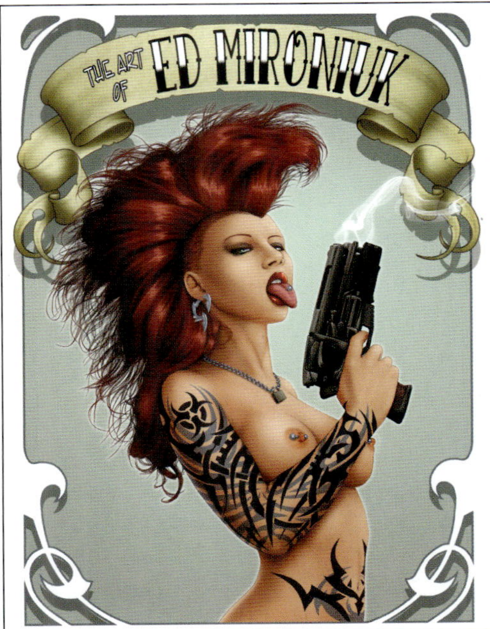

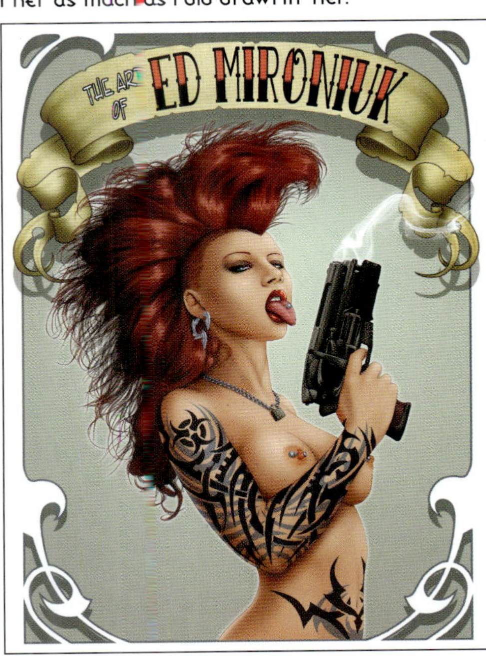

Credits where credits are due:

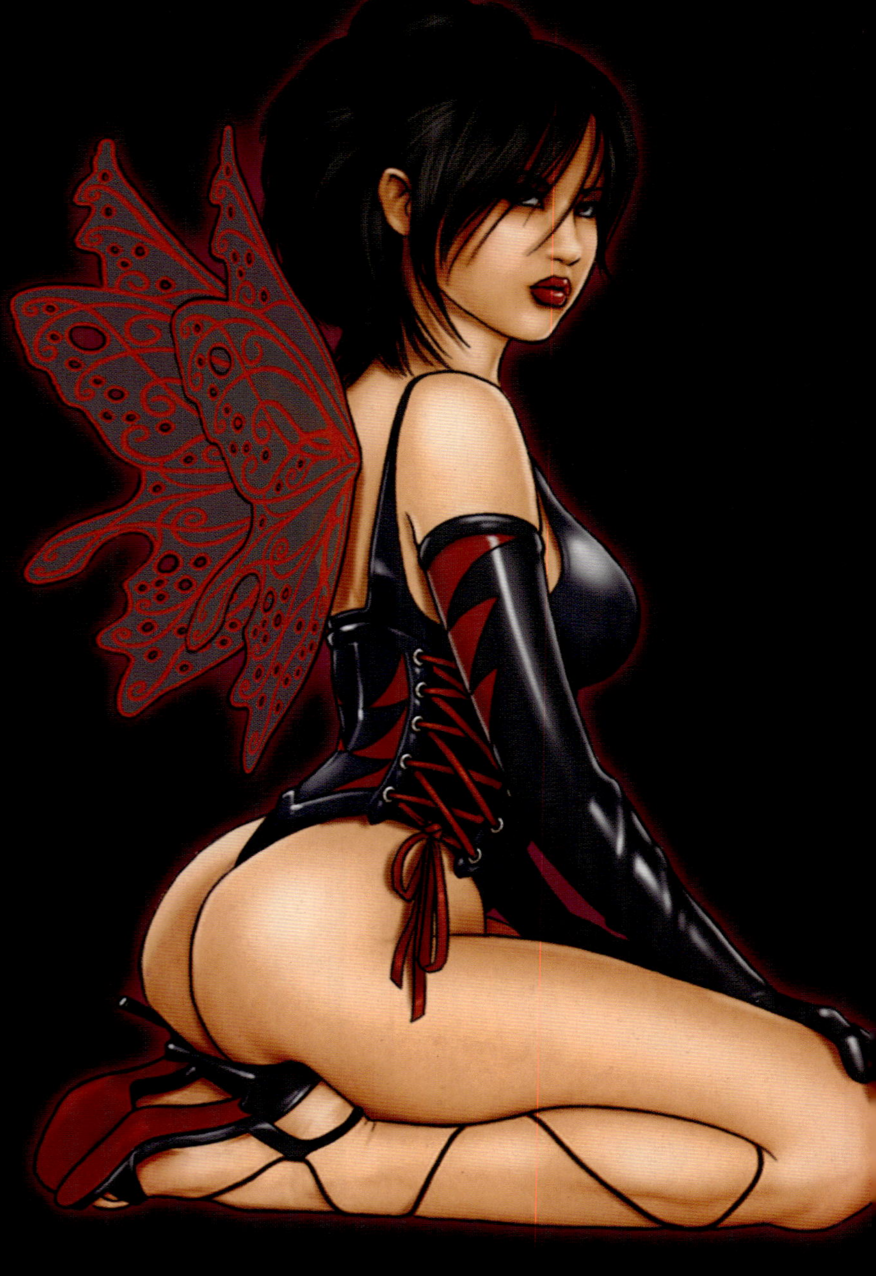

Inside Front Cover:
Title: Gash

Title Page:
Title: Beatnik Babe

Bio Page :
Mask by Bob Basset, Tattoo design by Papper & Penna, Ink pushed by Little Dragon at Last Rites.

Page 3:
Title: Keeriste

Page 5:
Title: Untitled

Page 5:
Title: Fascist

Page 6:
Title: Assassin Model: Masuimi Max Website: Iamtrouble.com

Page 7:
Title: Brandy Model: Brandy Durante
Website: myspace.com/tempestuous

Page 8:
Titles clockwise from left: AndroMohawk, Sex and Death in Television Town (Carlton Mellick III bookcover), Wasteland Warrior
Model: Black Widow Website: blackwidowsweb.org

Page 9:
Title: Love Slaves Model: Julie Strain Website: juliestrain.com

Page 10:
Titles: Gummi Gasmask and Cthulhu Nurse

Page 11:
Title: Apeshit (Carlton Mellick III bookcover)

Pages 12 and 13:
Title: Tattoo Magazine issue 153

Page 14:
Title: Frankenchick

Page 15:
Title: Cuddly Rigor Mortis Creature plush
Website: cuddlyrigormortis.com

Page 16:
Title: Cuddly Rigor Mortis Gimp plush

Page 17:
Title: Cuddly Rigor Mortis Devil plush

Page 18:
Title: Cthulhu Crapper

Page 19:
Title: Joan of the Apocalypse

Page 20:
Title: Tattoo Flash issue 96

Page 21:
Title: clockwise from top; Tattoo Magazine Issue 237, Tattoo Magaine issue 132, Flash Magazine issue 91

Page 22:
Title: Tattoo Magazine issue 227

Page 23:
Title: Tattoo Magazine issue 190

Page 24:
Title: Tattoo Magazine issue 179 Model: Dana Dark

Page 25:
Left Title: Tattoo Magazine issue 166, Right Title: Eightballed

Page 26:
Titles clockwise from top left: Tattoo Magazine issue 155, Tattoo Magazine issue 215, Tattoo Magazine issue 144, Tattoo Magazine issue 207

Page 27:
Title: Tattoo Magazine issue 233

Page 28:
Titles clockwise from top: Tattoo Magazine issue 185, Flash Magazine issue 68, Tattoo Magazine issue 200

Page 29:
Title: Tattoo Magazine issue 190

Page 30:
Title: Tattoo Magazine issue 228

Page 31:
Titles clockwise from top: Split-tat, Gasmask Geisha, Nihon Kaiju

Pages 32 and 33:
Title: Kumimonster Model: Kumi Website: kumimonster.com

Page 33:
Titles clockwise from top left: Poo-Peep, Hawaiian Hunnie, Neko, Metalhead

Page 34:
Title: Shiny Pussy Model: Karina

Page 35:
Top Title: Mistress Xotica, Bottom Title: Ashley Renee
Website: ashleyrenee.com

Page 36:
Title: Genitorturers Model: Gen Website: genitorturers.com

Page 37:
Title: We Won't Hurt You (But We Won't Go Away)
Models: SPiT LiKE THiS Website: spitlikethis.com

Page 38:
Titles clockwise from upper left:
Sasha Monet, Redhead Runway, Lil' Red, Catholicism

Page 39:
Top Title: Untitled, Bottom Title: Machinegun Babe
Model: Porsche Lynn Website : doiaz.com/

Page 40:
Title: Greasemonkey

Page 41:
Titles clockwise from top left: Kokoro Clean, Saltlick Santa, Xmas Ponygirls, Val N. Tyne

Page 42:
Title: Bloody Kokoro

Page 43:
Title: Oral Empire
Model: Tallgoddess Website: tallgoddess.com

Page 44:
Title: Adoration of the Hot Wings

Page 48:
Title: Dark Faerie

Back Cover:
Title: Mistress Mink